Stamboul Sketches

Stamboul Sketches

JOHN FREELY

with photographs by SEDAT PAKAY

and an afterword by MAUREEN FREELY

London

First published by Redhouse Press, Istanbul in 1974
This edition published by Eland Publishing Ltd
61 Exmouth Market, London ECIR 4QL in 2014

Copyright © John Freely 2014
Photographs throughout
by Sedat Pakay © Sedat Pakay 2014
John Freely has asserted his right under
the Copyright, Designs and Patents Act 1988
to be identified as the author of this work

ISBN 978 1 78060 056 7

Cover Image: Girl holding bread © Sedat Pakay
Text set in Great Britain by Antony Gray
Printed in Spain by GraphyCems, Navarra

Contents

For Toots

Introduction

'Though so many countries and cities have been minutely described by geographers and historians yet this my residence of Constantinople remains undescribed.' So said Sultan Murat IV to an assembly of scholars in the year 1638, as quoted by the contemporary Turkish traveller Evliya Efendi. This imperial complaint eventually led Evliya to write his own account of life in Istanbul during Murat's reign and those of his immediate successors. Evliya's description of the city is contained in two volumes of his *Seyahatname*, or *Narrative of Travels*, which he completed in about 1680. Many books have been written about Istanbul since then, but nothing which is comparable to Evliya's narrative, which recreates the colourful spectacle of life in the capital of the Ottoman Empire in the closing years of its golden age.

For Evliya was superbly equipped and situated to be the chronicler of that most fascinating period in the city's history. He was in his time a soldier, sailor, diplomat, historian, müezzin, goldsmith, writer, poet, singer, musician, and, above all, a traveller; equally at home in throne-room or taverna; an intimate of sultans and mighty pashas; a friend of poets, divines and sainted idiots; a comrade of common soldiers and humble workmen; familiar with all the exotic avenues and arcane byways of Istanbul life; his keen eye always looking for the curious sight, the odd character, the pleasurable walk or the panoramic view; his musician's ear listening for the sound of a street-hawker's cry, the melodies of a dervish song, the ditty of a drunken sailor; his gourmet's taste seeking out the most delicious food in town, and, although he claimed to be abstemious, the finest wines; his sharp nose sniffing out the earthy odours of Istanbul trade and commerce. Thereby he became a peripatetic encyclopaedia of the street-lore and folk history of his beloved city. Much has happened here in the past three centuries, but when we compare contemporary Istanbul with Evliya's town we see that its basic character has not really changed. Although the eunuchs and the Janissaries have gone, the sights and sounds and smells in the streets of Istanbul are much the same as those which Evliya records in the *Seyahatname*.

My own book is an attempt to evoke the spirit of the Istanbul that I have known, just as Evliya did for the city of his day. I have tried to do this through a series of brief sketches of Stamboul scenes. (I have here used the old-fashioned name of the city, as seeming more appropriate for the atmosphere I have tried to create.) Evliya Efendi appears and reappears throughout these sketches, for in his *Seyahatname* he touches on virtually every aspect of the city's life. So in my own wanderings through Stamboul I have constantly had him by my side, he comparing his town with mine, like an eccentric companion-guide. And I have often interwoven my narrative with that of Evliya Efendi, trying to bridge the gulf of years that separates his time from ours, so as to reveal something of the continuity of human experience which seems to exist in this ancient city.

These sketches were written over the course of the dozen years during which we have lived in Stamboul, and so many of them may now seem somewhat dated. For the scene has changed, and many of the characters have departed, some never to return. You will search in vain for the Albanian Flower-Pedlar and the Grandfather of Cats; Nazmi's Café and the Taverna Boem have closed their doors for ever; and some of our street-poets and wandering minstrels now sing and play here no more. Nevertheless I have made no attempt to update the sketches, for they and the photos by Sedat Pakay are a picture of the city we knew and loved in years past, the old Stamboul of our memories.

I would like to express my appreciation to William Edmonds of Redhouse Press for his help and encouragement in putting together *Stamboul Sketches*. Thanks are also due to Michael Cain for editorial work, and to Alan and Sue Ovenden, and Sara Rau for many helpful suggestions.

J. F., ISTANBUL, NOVEMBER 1ST 1973

Child standing in front of the Byzantine city walls

1

Evliya's Dream

Evliya, the son of Dervish Mehmet, was born in Stamboul on the tenth of Muharrem in the year after the Hegira 1020 (AD 1611) in the reign of Ahmet I. As Evliya writes in the *Seyahatname*, in the section entitled Anecdotes of the Youth of the Author, 'At the time when my mother was lying in with me, the humble Evliya, no fewer than seventy holy men were assembled at our house. At my birth the sheikh of the Mevlevi dervishes took me into his arms, threw me into the air, and catching me again, said, "May this boy be exalted in life!" ' After relating other anecdotes concerning these scholars and divines and the comments they made at the time of his birth, Evliya concludes with this characteristic statement: 'The short subject of this long discussion is to show that I, the humble Evliya, was favoured with the particular attention of these saints and holy men.'

Evliya came from an old and distinguished Turkish family which traced its lineage back to Sheikh Ahmet Yesov, who was the teacher of Hadji Bekta, the founder of the Bektaşi order of dervishes. Evliya's father had been Standard-Bearer in the army of Süleyman the Magnificent, and was at the Sultan's side when he died at the siege of Sziget in 1566. During the reign of Ahmet I, Dervish Mehmet became Chief of the Goldsmiths, a trade to which Evliya was apprenticed when he was a young man. His uncle and patron, Melek Ahmet Paşa, was a Grand Vezir in the reign of Murat IV (1623–40) and Evliya accompanied him on many of his missions and campaigns. His grandfather, Yavuz Ersinan, was Standard-Bearer in the army of Sultan Mehmet II and was present when Constantinople fell to the Turks in 1453. (Those two generations of Evliya's family span at least two centuries; either his forebears were incredibly long-lived or the intervening ancestors were foreshortened in the telescope of Evliya's imagination.)

After the Conquest, Yavuz Ersinan was allotted a plot of land in Unkapanı (the Flour Store), the district around the Stamboul shore of the present-day Atatürk Bridge. The mosque which he founded at that time, about 1455, is still standing and in use; it is probably the oldest surviving mosque in the city. It is called Sağrıcılar Camii, the Mosque of the Leather-Workers, after the artisans who have practised their trade in that neighbourhood for centuries. When Yavuz Ersinan died he was buried in the garden behind his mosque, and his moss-covered tomb-stone can still be seen there today. But the family homestead in which Evliya was born has vanished without a trace.

When he was six years old Evliya was enrolled in the school of Hamid Efendi in the section called Fil Yokuşu, the Path of the Elephant. (The street from which this section takes its name is still in existence, winding up from the shore of the Golden Horn to the heights above Unkapanı.) Evliya studied in Hamid Efendi's school for seven years, during which his tutor was Evliya Mehmet Efendi, Chief Imam in the court of Sultan Murat IV. While there he studied calligraphy, music, grammar and the Koran, in the reading and singing of which he particularly excelled. After leaving Hamid Efendi's school Evliya continued his studies with Evliya Mehmet Efendi, who appears to have given him a remarkably broad education. As Evliya once remarked to Murat IV: 'I am versed in seventy-two sciences; does your majesty wish to hear something of Persian, Arabic, Syriac, Greek or Turkish? Something of the different tunes of music, or poetry in various measures?' To which the Sultan replied: 'What a boasting fellow this is! Is he a Revani (a prattler), and is this all nonsense, or is he capable of performing all that he says?' We have only Evliya's own testimony to prove that he was no idle boaster, but an imaginative elaborator of the truth.

When Evliya was about twenty years old, so he tells us, he began making excursions in the vicinity of Istanbul and thereby decided to become a traveller. 'It was in the time of the illustrious reign of Murat IV that I began to think of extensive travels, in order to escape from the power of my father, mother and brethren. Forming a design of travelling over the whole earth, I entreated God to give me health for my body and faith for my soul. I sought the conversations of dervishes, and when I heard a description of the seven climates and of the four quarters of the earth, I became still more anxious to see the world, to visit the Holy Land, Cairo, Damascus, Mecca and Medina, and to prostrate myself on the purified soil of the places where the Prophet, the glory of all creatures, was born and died.'

With that hope Evliya prayed for divine guidance, a request which was eventually granted to him on his twenty-first birthday. He writes of how he fell asleep that night in his father's house and dreamt that he was in the nearby mosque of Ahi Çelebi. No sooner had he arrived there, in his dream, than the doors of the mosque opened and a brilliant crowd entered, all saying the morning prayer. Evliya tells us that he was lost in astonishment at the sight of this colourful assembly and that he looked upon his neighbour and said: 'May I ask, my lord, who you are, and what is your illustrious name?' His neighbour answered and said that he was Sa'd Vakkas, one of the ten evangelists and the patron of archers. Evliya kissed the hand of Sa'd Vakkas and asked further: 'Who are the refulgent multitude on my right hand?' 'They are all blessed saints and pure souls, the spirits of the followers of the Prophet,' answered Sa'd Vakkas, and then told Evliya that the Prophet himself, along with his grandsons Hasan and Hüseyin, were expected in the mosque at any moment to perform the morning service. No sooner had Sa'd Vakkas said this than flashes of lightning burst from the doors of the mosque and the room filled with a crowd of saints and martyrs. 'It was the Prophet!' Evliya writes, 'overshadowed by his green banner, covered by his green veil, carrying his staff in his right hand, his sword girt on his thigh, with the Imam Hasan on his right side and the Imam Hüseyin on his left. As he placed his right foot on the threshold he cried out, "Bismillah!" and throwing off his veil, said, "Health unto thee, O my people!" The whole assembly answered: "Unto thee be health, O prophet of God, Lord of the Nations!" ' Evliya tells us that he trembled in every limb, but still he was able to give a detailed description of the Prophet's appearance, saying that it agreed exactly with that given in the *Halþehi Khakani*: 'The veil on his face was a white shawl and his turban was formed of a white sash with twelve folds; his mantle was of camel's hair inclining to yellow; on his neck he wore a yellow woollen shawl. His boots were yellow and in his turban was stuck a toothpick.'

Evliya then tells us that the Prophet advanced to the mihrab of the mosque, struck his knees with his right hand, and commanded Evliya to take the lead in saying the morning prayers. Evliya did so and the Prophet followed by reciting the Fatihah, the first chapter of the Koran, along with other verses. After other prayers were pronounced by Evliya and Belal, the first müezzin of Islam, the morning prayers were concluded. 'The service was closed with a general cry of "Allah!" which very nearly woke me from my sleep,' Evliya writes. He then goes on to tell of how Sa'd Vakkas took him by the hand and escorted him into the Prophet's presence, saying, 'Thy loving and faithful servant Evliya entreats thy intercession.' Evliya, weeping in his excitement and confusion, kissed the Prophet's hands and received his blessings, along with the assurance that his desire to travel would be fulfilled. The Prophet then repeated the Fatihah, followed by all of his sainted companions, after which Evliya went round and kissed their hands, receiving from each his blessings. 'Their hands were perfumed with musk, ambergris, spikenard, sweet-basil, violets and carnations; but that of the Prophet himself smelt of nothing but saffron and roses, felt when touched as if it had no bones, and was as soft as cotton. The hands of the other prophets had the odour of quinces, that of Abu Bekr had the fragrance of lemons, Omar's smelt like ambergris, Osman's like violets, Ali's like jasmine, Hasan's like carnations, and Hüseyin's like white roses . . . Then the Prophet himself pronounced the parting salutation from the mihrab, after which he advanced towards the door and the whole illustrious assembly, giving me various greetings and blessings, went out of the mosque.'

The last to leave was Sa'd Vakkas, who took the quiver from his belt and gave it to Evliya, saying, 'Go, be victorious with thy bow and arrow; be in God's keeping, and receive from me the good tidings that thou

Children playing in Sülemaniye Street

shalt visit the tombs of all the prophets and holy men whose hands thou hast now kissed. Thou shalt travel through the whole world and be a marvel among men.' Then Sa'd Vakkas kissed Evliya's hand and departed from the mosque, leaving Evliya alone at the end of his dream.

'When I awoke,' writes Evliya, 'I was in great doubt whether what I had seen was a dream or reality, and I enjoyed for some time the beatific contemplations which filled my soul. Having afterwards performed my ablutions and offered up the morning prayer, I crossed over from Constantinople to the suburb of Kasımpaşa and consulted the interpreter of dreams, İbrahim Efendi, about my vision. From him I received the comfortable news that I would become a great traveller, and after making my way through the world, with the intercession of the Prophet, would close my career by being admitted into Paradise. I then retired to my humble abode, applied myself to the study of history, and began a description of my birthplace, Istanbul, that envy of kings, the celestial haven and stronghold of Macedonia.'

And so Evliya began the travels which eventually took him all over the Ottoman Empire, which at that time extended from central Persia to Gibraltar and from southern Egypt to the frontiers of Russia. He also accompanied the Turkish Embassy to Vienna in 1664, after which he travelled widely in northern and western Europe, returning by way of Poland and the Crimea. He took part in many military campaigns, the first of which was the siege and capture of Erivan in Persia by Murat IV in 1635, and he claims to have fought in twenty-two battles. But after each of these journeys he returned to Stamboul, and the largest part of his extant work is concerned with a description of his native city, its people and their life. He tells us that he travelled for forty years, passed through the countries of eighteen monarchs, and heard one hundred and forty-seven languages, but that nothing which he saw on his journeys compared in beauty or interest with his birthplace. He finally seems to have settled down in the Thracian city of Edirne, where he spent the closing decade of his life, dying there in about 1680 at the age of seventy. Evliya is thought to have spent those last years completing the *Seyahatname*, after the completion of those travels which had in fact taken him through 'the seven climates and the four quarters of the earth'.

But one wonders why Evliya left Stamboul as his life was drawing to a close. Perhaps, like so many writers before and after his time, he may have felt it necessary to escape from the pleasant company of his friends in order to get on with his work. But how Stamboul must have missed Evliya when he left for the last time, and how Evliya must have missed Stamboul.

The base of the Egyptian Obelisk in the Hippodrome

2

Talismans

Evliya Efendi begins his *Seyahatname* by giving what he calls 'an account of the ancient city and seat of Empire of the Macedonian Greeks, the well-guarded Constantinople, the envy of all the kings of the Land of Islam'. Evliya's version of the city's foundation is, as we might expect, fabulous. He informs us that 'all the ancient Greek historians are agreed that it was first built by Solomon, son of David, 1600 years before the birth of the Prophet. They say he caused a lofty palace to be erected by Genii, on the spot now called Saray Point, in order to please the daughter of Saidun, sovereign of Feridun, an island in the Western Ocean.'

At the time when Evliya was writing his description of the city, in the middle of the seventeenth century, memories of the Byzantine Empire had all but taken on the quality of legend. Aside from perhaps a score of churches, most of them by then converted into mosques, there remained in the city only some scattered ruins of imperial Byzantium. And so, in his customary way, Evliya invested these ruins with fabulous histories, claiming that many of them were magical talismans which had since antiquity protected the city of Constantinople. Many of Evliya's supposed talismans are still standing today, although, from the condition of the modern town, they would seem to have lost their magical powers. But there are those of us for whom some magic still remains, for these talismanic ruins can evoke the fabled past of Byzantium, especially with Evliya Efendi at one's side.

Pride of place among these ancient monuments should perhaps be given to the Column of Constantine, although Evliya ranks it only second among the talismans of the city. This column was dedicated by Constantine the Great on May 11 in the year AD330, the day on which

Constantinople officially became the capital of the Roman Empire. The column, which was originally surmounted by a statue of the Emperor himself, stood in the centre of the Forum of Constantine, now a minor intersection on the Avenue of the Janissaries. The identity of the column and its historical significance were almost forgotten by Evliya's time. Nevertheless, the name of Constantine the Great still seems to have been associated with it, as we can see from Evliya's description: 'In the Poultry Market there is a needle-like column formed of many pieces of red emery stone, a hundred royal cubits high. This was damaged by the earthquake which occurred on the two nights during which the Pride of the World (Mohammed) was called into existence; but the builders girt it round with iron hoops, as thick as a man's thigh, so that it is still firm and standing. It was erected 140 years before the era of Iskender (Alexander the Great). Kostantin (Constantine the Great) placed a talisman on top of it in the form of a starling, which once a year clapped its wings and brought all the birds in the air to the place, each with three olives in its beak and talons.'

The second of the city's surviving imperial columns, the Column of Marcian, stands in the centre of a quiet little crossroads near Beyazıt Square. This column, huge as it is, was completely lost sight of for centuries and almost forgotten, for it stood in the garden of a private house. But then, in the great fire of 1908, the surrounding houses were burned to the ground and the column was once again exposed to public view. (Do we detect here the crime of an antiquarian-arsonist?) On the pedestal of the column there are still visible the figures of two Nikes in high relief; one of them holds a basket decorated with a cross and myrtle leaves. Below these figures we can make out the outlines of an inscription in Latin. It reads: 'Tatianus Decius raised this column for the Emperor Marcian. December 450–July 452.' The Turks call this column Kız Taşi, or the Maiden's Column, because of the reliefs of the two Winged Victories which appear on the pedestal. This has led them to confuse the Kız Taşi with the famous Column of Venus, which also stood in this neighbourhood; this column reputedly possessed the power of being able to distinguish true virgins from false ones. Evliya

Efendi listed the Maiden's Column as the third of the city's talismans, giving this brief description: 'At the head of the Saddler's Bazaar, on the summit of a column stretching to the skies, there is a chest of white marble in which the unlucky daughter of King Puzantin lies buried; and to preserve her remains from ants and serpents was this column made a talisman.' Talismanic protector of a dead princess and indicator of false virgins; this is indeed a fabulous column!

Of the other imperial columns which once studded the city only a solitary but fascinating fragment remains. This is the base of the Column of Arcadius, which stands in the lovely old district of Samatya. This column was erected by the Emperor Arcadius in 402 to commemorate his victories over the Goths and Visigoths. At the top of the column there was an enormous Corinthian capital surmounted by a colossal equestrian statue of Arcadius, placed there in 421 by his son, Theodosius the Lesser. This statue was eventually toppled from the column and destroyed in 704. The column itself remained standing for another thousand years, until it was deliberately demolished in 1715, when it was feared that it might fall on the neighbouring houses. All that remains today is the base of the monument, a battered mass of blackened stone completely overgrown with ivy and wedged in between a bakery and an old wooden tenement. Evliya, who saw the column before it was destroyed, numbered it first in his list of the city's talismans. After describing the column itself, he gives this account of its talismanic powers: 'On the summit of the column there was anciently a fair-cheeked figure of one of the beauties of the age, which once a year gave a sound, on which several hundred thousand kinds of birds, after flying round and round the image, fell down to earth and being caught by the people of Rum (Rome), provided them with an abundant meal. After, in the age of Kostantin, the monks placed bells upon it, in order to give alarm on the approach of an enemy. Subsequently, on the birth of the Prophet, there was a great earthquake by which the statue and all the bells on top of the figure were thrown topsy-turvy and the column itself broke into pieces; but being formed by the talismanic art it could not be destroyed and part of it remains as an extraordinary spectacle to this day.'

Evliya tells us that another half-dozen talismans are to be found in Altımermer, the district of the Six Marbles. The eponymous marbles, presumably columns, from which the district takes its name probably stood in or near the enormous Roman reservoir which is located in that area. This reservoir, anciently called the cistern of Mocius, was constructed towards the end of the fifth century, during the reign of Arcadius. Though the columns which Evliya describes are no longer to be found in the reservoir itself, there is a tradition which holds that they are the ones which now stand in the colonnade of the nearby mosque of Hekimoğlu Ali Paşa. Evliya outdoes himself in describing these talismanic columns, telling us that 'every one of them was an observatory, made by some of the ancient sages'. The sages with whom Evliya associates these talismans are a most formidable group, namely: Hippocrates, Socrates, Pythagoras, Plato, Aristotle, Galen and King Philip of Macedonia, who would surely be surprised to find himself in the company of such distinguished intellectuals. On one of the columns stood a brass fly which, by its incessant humming, drove away all flies from the city, and on the second stood the figure of a gnat, which performed a similar service. On a third column stood the figure of a wolf which protected the flocks of the city from the attacks of real wolves. On a fourth column there was the figure of a stork which once a year let out a cry, whereupon all the storks within the city fell dead. Evliya tells us that this is the reason why storks do not build their nests within the city walls but prefer the suburb of Eyüp, on the upper reaches of the Golden Horn. These last two talismans would appear to be effective even now in protecting the town, for wolves are never seen in the streets of Stamboul and storks still nest only in Eyüp. But in warm weather the town swarms with flying insects, and so the brass fly and gnat must have disappeared or lost their powers. As Evliya tells us: 'Wonderful talismans were destroyed, they say, in the time of that asylum of apostleship (Mohammed) and are now buried in the earth.'

The fifth and sixth talismans in Altımermer performed services of a different kind, according to Evliya: 'On one of these columns were the figures of a youth and his mistress in close embrace. Whenever there

Gypsy houses leaning against Byzantine walls

was any coolness or quarrelling between man and wife, they were sure that very night to have their afflicted hearts restored by love if either of them went and embraced this column, which was moved by the spirit of Aristotle ... Two figures in tin were placed on another column; one was a decrepit old man, bent double; and opposite to it was a camel-lip, sour-faced hag, no straighter than her companion. When a man and wife did not lead a happy life together a separation was sure to take place if either embraced this column, which was placed there by the sage Galen.'

Although Evliya originally told us that there were six talismans at Altımermer, we find in reading his account that there were actually seven. This extra talisman was a brazen cock placed there by Socrates. As Evliya informs us: 'This cock clapped its wings and crowed once in every twenty-four hours, and on hearing it all the cocks in Istanbul started to crow. And it is a fact that all the cocks there crow earlier than those of other places, setting up their *ku-kirri-ku* at midnight, and thus warning the sleepy and the forgetful of the approach of dawn and the hour of prayer.' We are told by a sleepy and forgetful friend in this neighbour-hood that the brazen cock of Socrates must still be active, for he is awakened long before dawn each day by cocks crowing in the cistern of Altımermer. The cistern, which has been dry for centuries, now serves as a fruit orchard and vegetable garden. A picturesque farm village has grown up within the cistern, a curiously rural community isolated in its vernal, subterranean world, providing a pleasant contrast with the densely populated urban slum around it. The tops of the smoking chimneys, the minaret of the village mosque, and the upper branches of the flowering fruit trees reach up barely to the level of the surrounding streets. Evliya Efendi tells us that we can descend into this little arcadia down a stone staircase called the Forty Steps, although, as he hastens to add, the actual number of steps is fifty-four. The Turks call this lovely place Çukurbostan, or the Sunken Garden.

Three of the most fascinating of Evliya's talismans stand on the site of the ancient Hippodrome, reminding us of the illustrious past of that famous arena. The site of the Hippodrome is today a quiet, tree-shaded park before the mosque of Sultan Ahmet. The street which borders this park follows exactly the course of the ancient racetrack. The Kathisma, or royal enclosure, was located at the northern end of the arena, where now reeks a public toilet. Of the many monuments and works of art which once adorned the Hippodrome only three remain, standing in line along what was once the *spina*, the longitudinal axis of the arena. They have survived, as Evliya would say, because they were fashioned by the talismanic art.

The first of these monuments, beginning at the southern end of the arena, is a huge obelisk of squared stones called the Colossus. Evliya numbered this obelisk as the fifteenth of the city's talismans, describing it in his inimitable style: 'It was constructed by Kostantin's order of various coloured stones, collected from the 300,000 cities of which he was king, and designed to be an eternal monument to his power, and at the same time a talisman. Through the middle of it there ran a thick iron axis, round which the various coloured stones were placed, and they were all kept together by a magnet as large as the cupola of a public bath, which was fixed on its summit.'

The second in line of the ancient monuments in the Hippodrome is the Serpentine Column. This strange column has had a most interesting past. The three intertwined bronze serpents which form the column once served as the base of a golden trophy which stood in the Temple of Apollo at Delphi. This trophy was originally presented to the temple by the thirty-one Greek cities which together defeated the Persians at the battle of Plataea in 479 BC. The column was brought from Delphi by Constantine the Great and eventually erected in the Hippodrome. The three serpent heads were broken off and lost sometime after the Turkish Conquest in 1453. Evliya Efendi has something to tell us about this in his description of the Serpentine Column, which he numbers seventeenth among the city's talismans: 'A sage named Surendeh, who flourished in the days of error under King Puzantin, set up a brazen image of a triple-headed dragon in order to destroy all serpents, lizards, scorpions and suchlike poisonous reptiles. It remained uninjured till Sultan Selim II, surnamed the Drunkard, knocked off with his mace the lower part of that head of the dragon which looks to the west. Serpents then made their appearance on the western side of the city, and since that time have become very common in every part of it. If, moreover, the remaining heads should be destroyed, Istanbul will be completely eaten up by vermin.'

The two remaining heads were lost after Evliya's time and his dire prediction came to be fulfilled, for Stamboul today is literally overrun by vermin. But one of the missing serpent heads has been rediscovered and is now exhibited in the Archaeological Museum. In view of Evliya's warning, it is imperative that this talismanic fragment be restored to its proper place without delay.

The third of the Hippodrome's surviving monuments is the Egyptian Obelisk, which stands in the centre of the *spina*. It was originally commissioned by the Pharaoh Thutmose III, who erected it at Deir el Bahri in upper Egypt around 1550 BC. The obelisk was brought to Constantinople and erected in its present location by Theodosius the Great in the year 390. Evliya lists the Egyptian Obelisk as sixteenth among the talismans of the city. He tells us that 'this is an obelisk of red coloured stone, covered with various sculptures which foretell the fortune of the city. It was erected in the time of Yanko ibn Madiyan, who is represented on it sitting on his throne.'

The sculptures of which Evliya speaks are carved in low relief on the four sides of the pedestal which supports the obelisk. They are of particular interest because they show us something of what the Hippodrome was like fifteen centuries ago. One panel shows the Emperor Theodosius supervising the erection of the obelisk. Another shows the Emperor and his family looking down into the arena where a group of captives offers tribute to them. In a third panel of the obelisk the royal family is shown seated in the Kathisma watching a chariot race, and in the last panel Theodosius holds a laurel wreath and prepares to crown the winner. Below the Kathisma we see the faces of the crowd in the stadium; their features, like those of the royal family, are worn and broken by the centuries. At the bottom of this panel we can make out the figures of a line of female dancers performing in the arena. Behind the dancers three musicians are playing in accompaniment; one seems to be working a laterna, another is playing on a stringed instrument, and the third is blowing on a double Lydian flute. The dancers have their arms linked together and their leader has her free hand raised in the air. Looking at their graceful postures we seem to recognise the movements of the *kesapico*, one of the oldest of all Greek folk-dances. During the days of Byzantium the *kesapico* was performed annually in the Hippodrome on Easter Monday, and it is still danced today in the few Greek tavernas which remain in Istanbul. Looking at the worn frieze of dancers on the pedestal, we are reminded of the antiquity of all practices in this talisman-protected town.

The Hall of the Black Eunuchs in the Harem

3

Evliya and the Sultan

In Book I of the *Seyahatname* we read an 'Account of the humble Evliya's admission into the imperial Harem of Murat IV, and of some pleasant conversations which he enjoyed with the Sultan in the year AH1046 (AD1635)'. Evliya's story of his meeting with the Sultan and of the events which followed is one of the most fascinating sections of the *Seyahatname*. For Evliya became one of Murat's *musahibs*, or favourites, and was privileged to observe the palace from within and to know the Sultan intimately as a human being. Evliya's account of the months which he spent in the Saray thus brings the old palace back to life once again, and peoples it with the ghosts of its departed inhabitants.

Evliya first came to the Sultan's notice on the sacred night of Kadir in 1635, about four years after his vision of the Prophet. On that evening Evliya was serving as a müezzin in Haghia Sophia and, in the Sultan's presence, began to recite the entire Koran from memory. This so impressed Murat that he sent two of his aides to fetch Evliya and bring him to his side. Accordingly, they proceeded to the müezzin's gallery. There, before the eyes of the entire congregation, they placed a golden turban on Evliya's head and led him by the hand to the Sultan's loge. Here is Evliya's account of his first audience with Murat: 'On beholding the dignified countenance of Sultan Murat, I bowed and kissed the ground. The Emperor received me very graciously, and, after salutations, asked me in how many hours I could repeat the Koran. I said, if it please God, and if I proceed at a rapid pace, I could repeat it in seven hours, but if I do it moderately, without much alternation of voice, I can accomplish it in eight hours. The Sultan then said, "Please God, let him be admitted into the number of my intimate associates in the room of the deceased Musa." He then gave me two or three handfuls of gold, which altogether amounted to 623 pieces.'

At the conclusion of the service Evliya was escorted to Topkapı Sarayı and was informed that he would become a member of the Inner Service, those who served in the Sultan's own household. When he arrived at the palace Murat's attendants greeted him and prepared him for his formal introduction to the Sultan. 'They invested me with an embroidered robe, put an amber-scented tuft of artificial hair upon my head, and wishing me a thousand blessings told me that I wore the crown of happiness.' Afterwards two mutes came and led him to the throne-room, where two of Murat's pages instructed him as to his behaviour in the Sultan's presence. Then, as Evliya writes, 'The Emperor made his appearance, like the rising sun, by the door leading to the inner Harem. He saluted the forty pages of the Inner Service and all the *musahibs*, who returned the salutation with prayers for his prosperity. The Emperor having with great dignity seated himself on one of the thrones, I kissed the ground before him and trembled all over. The next moment, nonetheless, I complimented him with some verses that most fortunately came to my mind.'

And after he had recited these verses, Evliya matched wits with the Sultan and his favourites, recited poetry for them, played upon the tambourine and danced like a dervish before the throne, and then sang a plaintive love song which reduced Murat to tears. When he recovered his composure the Sultan immediately directed that Evliya be admitted into the company of his *musahibs*. This singular audience ended when the call to prayer was heard, whereupon, as Evliya writes, 'The Emperor ordering me to assist the müezzin, I flew like a peacock to the top of the staircase and began to exclaim, "Ho, to good works!" '

Shortly afterwards Evliya was enrolled in the Palace School, that admirable institution which trained young men for careers in the various branches of the government and palace service. Something of the quality of life in the Saray at that time can be gathered from Evliya's description of his fellow pages in the Palace School, within what he called the Abode of Felicity: 'The privy chambers of the palace were occupied by three thousand pages, beautiful as Joseph, richly attired in shirts fragrant as roses, each having his place in the imperial service, where he was always ready to serve.'

After Evliya had been in the Palace School for some time, he accompanied the Sultan one day to Haghia Sophia, where he was noticed by his former teacher and namesake, the Chief Imam Evliya Efendi. The elder Evliya thereupon approached the Sultan and addressed him thus: 'My gracious Emperor, this boy, the darling of my heart, has not attended my lectures since the sacred night of Kadir, when you took him to the palace. He has already learned the whole of the Koran according to the seven readings; he is thoroughly acquainted with the Shatebi treatise on that subject, and was beginning the study of the fifteen readings. Allow him to perfect himself in these studies, after which he may return to your majesty's service.' Sultan Murat then reprimanded the old imam sternly, saying: 'Efendi! Do you suppose that our palace is a tavern or a den of robbers? Three thousand pages are there devoted night and day to the study of the sciences, besides attending the general lectures as well as those which your reverence delivers twice a week. He may attend your lectures as before; but I cannot leave him to your disposal, for he is a lively and intelligent youth, and must remain with me as my son.'

And so Evliya did for several months, enjoying the Sultan's favour and observing those parts of the palace and its life which were open to him. Unfortunately he makes no mention of the Harem, for that was closely guarded by the black eunuchs and forbidden even to the Sultan's companions. But from what we know of Murat, he cared little for the pleasures of the Harem, preferring the company of his *musahibs*. Evliya knew this well, and when he entertained the Sultan at his first audience his song was of Murat's beloved Musa, the favourite who had been murdered by the Janissaries when he first came to the throne. And although Musa had been dead for more than ten years, the Sultan wept when Evliya sang of him that night. 'I went out to meet my beloved Musa; he tarried and came not/Perhaps I missed him on the way . . . ' So sang Evliya to the bereaved Murat, and in that way himself became the Sultan's *musahib*.

Evliya seems to have been constantly at the Sultan's side during his tenure as *musahib*, and gives a detailed description of how Murat spent his days. Here, for example, is his account of the Sultan's weekly schedule of audiences in the throne-room, from which we learn something about the mind and heart of the man himself.

During the winter he regulated his audiences as follows:

On Friday he assembled all the divines, sheikhs and the readers of the Koran, and with them he disputed till morning on scientific subjects. Saturday morning was devoted to the singers who sang the İlâhi, the Na't, and other spiritual tunes. Sunday evening was appropriated to poets and reciters of romances. On Monday evening he had the dancing boys and the Egyptian musicians. This assembly sat until daybreak and resembled the musical feast of Hüseyin Bukhara. On Tuesday evenings he received the old experienced men who were upwards of seventy and with them he used to converse in the most familiar manner. On Wednesday he gave audience to the pious saints, and on Thursday to the dervishes. In the mornings he attended to the affairs of the Moslems. In such a manner did he watch over the affairs of the Ottoman states, that not even a bird could fly over them without his knowledge. But were we to describe all his excellent qualities we should fill another volume.

Evliya was also able to watch the Sultan at play, when he revealed another and appealing aspect of his extraordinarily varied nature. Here is Evliya's description of an amusing encounter he had one day with Murat, in the corridor outside the Sultan's bath:

One day the Emperor came out covered with perspiration from his hamam near the throne-room, saluted those present and said, 'Now I have had my bath.' 'May it be to your health', was the general reply. I said, 'My Emperor, you are now clean and comfortable, do not therefore oil yourself for wrestling today, especially since you have already exercised with others and your strength must be considerably reduced.' 'Now, have I no strength left?' said he. 'Let us see,' upon which he seized me like an eagle, raised me over his head and whirled me about as children do a top. I exclaimed, 'Do not let me fall, my Emperor, hold me fast!' He said, 'Hold fast yourself!' and continued to swing me around, until I cried out, 'For God's sake, my Emperor, cease, for I am quite giddy!' He then began to laugh, released me, and gave me forty-eight pieces of gold for the amusement which I had offered him. The Sultan subsequently stripped himself and wrestled with his Sword-Bearer, Melek Ahmet Ağa, and Musa Ağa, both remarkably stout men, and took them by their belts, lifted them over his head, and flung one of them to the right and the other to the left. It was I who on such occasions read the wrestler's prayer.

Sultan Murat proved to be a strong and able ruler and checked for a time the decline of the Ottoman Empire, which had begun after the death of Süleyman the Magnificent. He was the first sultan in nearly a century to lead his army into battle and was victorious in several campaigns, climaxed by the capture of Erivan in 1635 and of Baghdad in 1638. Evliya accompanied Murat on the first of these campaigns and was present when the Sultan made his triumphant return to Stamboul, leaving us this spirited account in the *Seyahatname*:

On the nineteenth of Rejab 1045 the illustrious Emperor made his entry into Constantinople with a splendour and magnificence which no tongue can describe or pen illustrate. The windows and roofs of the houses in every direction were crowded with people, who exclaimed, 'The blessing of God be upon thee O Conqueror! Welcome Murat! May thy victories be fortunate!' The Sultan was dressed in steel armour and had a threefold aigrette in his turban, stuck obliquely on one side in the Persian manner. He was mounted on a Noghai steed, followed by seven led horses of the Arab breed, decked out in embroidered trappings set with jewels. Emirguneh, the Khan of the Persians, walked on foot before him, whilst the band with cymbals, flutes, drums and fifes, played the airs of Afrasiab. The

Emperor looked with dignity on both sides of him, like a lion who has
seized his prey, and saluted his people as he went on, followed
by three thousand pages clad in armour. During this triumphal
procession to the palace all the ships at Saray Point fired salutes,
so that the sea seemed in a blaze. Afterwards the public criers
announced that seven days and nights were to be devoted to festivity
and rejoicing.

After the Baghdad campaign, the last great triumph of Ottoman arms,
Murat retired from the field and spent most of his time in the palace,
carousing in the company of his *musahibs*. During his last years he began
to drink heavily and at times behaved like a homicidal maniac, keeping
Stamboul in terror from his murderous rages. But even then, according
to Evliya, Murat could still be of a jovial disposition, a lover of music,
poetry and good fellowship, a brave and just ruler. As Evliya wrote of
Murat in the *Seyahatname*:

> I enjoyed the great favour of the Sultan, who relished a joke or a laugh
> as well as any plain dervish. But although he had the nature of a
> dervish, he was brave and intelligent. Neither the Ottoman nor any
> other dynasty of Moslem rulers ever produced a prince so athletic, so
> well-made, so much feared by his enemies, or so dignified as Sultan
> Murat. Though so cruel and bloodthirsty, he conversed with rich and
> poor without any mediator, and made his rounds day and night to
> be informed of the state of the poor, and to ascertain the price of
> provisions, for which purpose he often went into cook-shops and
> dined incognito. But no monarch was ever so guilty of so many violent
> deeds. The Emperor was also a good poet, and his *divan*, or collection
> of odes, ran to three hundred pages, but he died before he could
> complete it.

Sultan Murat IV died on February 9th in the year 1640, while the
Ottoman fleet was preparing for a campaign against Malta. He was
then not yet thirty years of age. According to Evliya, in the section
entitled *An Account of the Death of Sultan Murat*:

The standards were already raised preparatory to a new expedition, when the Emperor, enfeebled by sickness, found it impractical to set out. According to the Arabic text: 'Every one must perish,' and the Persian verse: 'If any person could remain forever on earth, Mohammed would have remained; if beauty could secure immortality, Joseph would not have died,' no one is exempt from destiny. And Sultan Murat being obedient to the call, 'Return to thy Lord,' bade farewell to this perishable world and entered on his journey to the everlasting kingdom. The whole of the Moslem kingdom was thrown into the deepest affliction and lamented his loss. Horses hung with black were let loose in the At Meydanı, where his majesty was buried close to his father, Sultan Ahmet . . . I have since heard from the pearl-shedding lips of my lord, Kara Mustafa, that had God spared Murat but six months longer, the whole of the infidels would have been reduced to the capitation tax.

The only buildings left in Topkapı Sarayı from the days of Sultan Murat IV are two handsome kiosks in the Fourth Court. They are called the Erivan Köşkü and the Bagdad Köşkü, and were built to commemorate the Sultan's two great victories. The loveliest of the two is the Bagdad Köşkü, which is said to be modelled after a building which he saw in that city after its capture. It is revealing of Murat's character that he thought the Persian kiosk to be the most splendid he had ever seen, and that he destroyed it and built one exactly like it in his palace. It is perhaps the most beautiful room in the whole Saray, and we can appreciate the pleasure that it must have given to Sultan Murat, in what would be the last year of his short life. We can still imagine Murat there reclining on a divan, surrounded by his *musahibs*, listening to Evliya Efendi singing a mournful love song. 'I went out to meet my beloved Musa; he tarried and came not/Perhaps I missed him on the way . . . '

Reenactment of a Janissary parade

4

The Procession of the Guilds

It is not until the second half of Book II of the *Seyahatname* that Evliya
finally begins his account 'of all the Guilds and Professions, Merchants
and Artisans, Shops and Various Occupations in this vast town of
Constantinople, with the Regulations handed down to them by their
Sheikhs or Ancients'. Evliya's account is based upon his observation of
the extraordinary public muster which was ordered in 1638 by Sultan
Murat IV, in preparation for his march upon Baghdad. As Evliya writes,
quoting the Sultan: ' "Dear companions, and you Mufti Yahya Efendi, if
it please God we will wrest Baghdad from the hands of the Persians, and
deliver from their heresy the tomb of the founder of our orthodox sect.
In order to assist me in our great expedition, I desire that all the guilds of
Constantinople, both large and small, shall repair to my imperial camp.
They shall exhibit the number of their men, shops and professions,
according to their old constitutions. They shall pass before the Alay
Köşkü with their Sheikhs and Chiefs, on foot and on horseback, playing
their eightfold music, so that I may see how many thousand men and
how many guilds there are. It shall be a procession the likes of which
was never seen before." '

It was indeed, according to Evliya's description of the parade, one of
the last of its kind ever to be seen in Stamboul. During Ottoman times
these imperial processions were held but once or twice a century. They
served as a kind of perambulatory census of the trade and commerce of
the city, often as part of the preparations for a great military campaign
such as that of Murat IV. The Sultan viewed his passing citizens from
the Alay Köşkü, the Kiosk of the Processions, a huge gazebo projecting
from the outer defence-wall of Topkapı Sarayı just opposite the Sublime

Porte. Seeing the kiosk today, we are reminded of the lively and colourful procession which passed before it in Evliya's day.

As Evliya describes it, the procession was led by the Çavuş, or Ushers, 'upon whom it is incumbent to collect and assemble the rest. Their patron is Malek Ushtur, who from having killed a dragon in China is vulgarly called Ejder (Dragon), but who got his name from having lost one of his eyes in battle. The Çavuş adorn their horses in honour of their patron with sea-horse bristles and various glittering ornaments, dress in brilliant stuffs, carry in their hand a musket, on their waist a sword, and on their head seven feathers like those of Simurq, and crying out with a voice like Modikarb and Malek Ushtur, put the columns of the army into motion.'

Evliya tells us that the procession was organised into fifty-seven sections and consisted of a thousand-and-one guilds, although the number of guilds which he actually describes is just seven hundred and thirty-five. Representatives of each of these guilds paraded in their characteristic costumes or uniforms, exhibiting on floats their various trades and enterprises, trying to outdo one another in amusing or amazing the Sultan and the other spectators.

All these guilds pass on wagons or on foot, with the instruments of their handicraft, and are busy with great noise at their work. The carpenters prepare wooden houses, the builders raise walls, the woodcutters pass with loads of trees, the sawyers pass sawing them, the masons whiten their shops, the chalk-makers crunch chalk and whiten their faces, playing a thousand tricks . . . The toy-makers of Eyüp exhibit on wagons a thousand trifles and toys for children to play with. In their train you see bearded fellows and men of thirty years of age, some dressed as children with hoods and bibs, some as nurses who care for them, while the bearded babies cry after play-things or amuse themselves with spinning tops or sounding little trumpets . . . The Greek fur-makers of the marketplace of Mahmut Paşa form a separate procession, with caps of bearskin and breeches of fur. Some are dressed from head to foot in lion's, leopard's and wolves' skin, with kalpaks of sable on their heads. Some dress again in skins, as wild men and savages, so that those who see them are afraid, each one being held by strong chains and led by six or seven people, while others are dressed as strange creatures with their feet apparently turned to the sky, while they walk with their real feet upon the ground . . . The Bakers pass working at their trade, some baking and throwing small loaves among the crowd. They also make for this occasion immense loaves, the size of the cupola of a hamam, covered with sesame and fennel; these loaves are carried on wagons which are dragged along by seventy to eighty pairs of oxen. No oven being capable of holding loaves of so large a size, they bake them in pits made for that purpose, where the loaf is covered from above with cinders, and from the four sides baked slowly by the fire. It is worth while to see it . . . These guilds pass before the Alay Köşkü with a thousand tricks and fits, which it is impossible to describe, and behind them walk their Sheikhs followed by their pages playing the eightfold Turkish music.

Evliya tells us that there were several disputes concerning precedence in the imperial procession. The first of these quarrels was between the Butchers and the Captains of the White Sea (the Mediterranean). The Captains, having heard that the Butchers were slated to pass before them, assembled together and presented a petition to the Sultan, saying that they would be subjected to everlasting shame if their eminent guild was forced to parade behind the 'blood-shedding' Butchers. Sultan Murat settled the dispute in favour of the Captains of the White Sea, issuing this imperial edict: 'Indeed, besides the fact that they supply the capital with provisions, they have also taken Noah for their protector. They are a respectable guild of men, who militate in God's ways against the Infidels, and are well-skilled in many sciences. They may also pass in great solemnity, and then be followed by the Butchers.'

And so the Captains of the White Sea were moved up in the order of the imperial procession, and proceeded to put on one of the most elaborate and spirited displays seen that day, according to Evliya.

The Captains of the Caravellas, Galleons and other ships, having fired from them a triple salute at Saray Point, pour all their men on shore, where they place on floats some hundred small boats and drag them along with cables, shouting 'Aya Mola!' In their boats are seen the finest cabin boys dressed in gold doing service to their masters, who make free with drinking. Music is played on all sides, the masts and oars are adorned with pearls and set with jewels, the sails are of rich stuffs and embroidered muslin, and on the top of each mast are a couple of boys whistling tunes of Silistria. Arriving at the Alay Köşkü they meet five or ten ships of the Infidels, with whom they engage in battle in the presence of the Emperor. Thus the show of a great fight is represented with the roaring of cannons, the smoke covering the sky. At last the Moslems becoming victors, they board the ships of the Infidels, take booty and chase the fine Frank boys, carrying them off from the old bearded Infidels, whom they put in chains. They upset the crosses of the Infidel flags and dragging the captured vessels astern of their own ships, they cry out the universal Moslem slogan of 'Allah! Allah!' . . . Never before the time of Sultan Murat IV was there seen so brilliant a union of mariners.

After the Captains of the White Sea had passed with their entourage, the Butchers once again attempted to join the line of march, but their place was disputed by the guild of the Egyptian Merchants. The adversaries assembled before the Alay Köşkü and once again the Sultan decided against the Butchers, 'to the great delight of the Egyptian Merchants, who, leaping for joy, passed immediately after the Captains of the White Sea'.

Then finally the Butchers were allowed to take their place in the procession, marching before the Men of the Slaughter-House and the Jewish Meat-Merchants, neither of whom would seem to have had any influence with the Sultan. 'The Butchers, who are almost all Janissaries, pass clad in armour on wagons, exposing to public view in their shops, adorned with rich stuffs and flowers, fat sheep of Karamania weighing from forty to fifty occas. They trace on their white flesh figures with saffron, gild their horns, cut them up with their large knives, and weighing them in yellow-coloured scales, cry: "Take the occa for an asper, take it my soul, it is an excellent roast dish." Thus chanting, they parade with their large knives and cutlasses, passing on foot in the procession.'

Still another quarrel over precedence took place between the Fish-Cooks and the Helvacıs, or sugar-bakers. As Evliya tells it:

The Emperor decided that the latter should go first, to the great annoyance of the Fish-Cooks, who appealed to their patron Jonah and blamed the Helvacıs, who reproached the Fish-Cooks, saying fish was very unwholesome and infatuating food. In proof they adduced what happened when the famous Yazıcı-zadeh Mohammed Efendi, the author of the *Mohammedieh*, sent his work in the year 847 (1443) to Balkh and Bukhara. When the doctors of those two towns were told that the author had written it on the seashore shut up in a cave, they decided that he could never have eaten a fish, because a man who eats much fish loses his intellect and never could have compiled so valuable a work. The disciples of the author averred the fact that neither he, his father, nor his grandfather had ever eaten fish. To this reproach the Helvacıs added the praise of the Helva contained in the Koran, and quoted the Prophet, who once said: 'The faithful are sweet, the wicked sour.' Having put forth their claims in this way in the Emperor's presence, they carried the votes of the whole assembly that the precedence was due to them rather than to the Fish-Cooks, and accordingly obtained the imperial diploma.

Thus the Helvacıs took their place in the procession 'fitting up their shops on litters with all kinds of sweets, which bring water into the mouths of the boys of the town, who devour them with their eyes. They exhibit on litters different kinds of confectionaries in basins, and perfume the brains of the spectators with amber scent. They produce at this public exhibition trees of sugar with sweets upon them, an admirable show! Behind them walks the Chief Confectioner of the Saray, followed by the troops of the confectioners playing the eightfold Turkish music.'

So they passed before the Alay Köşkü in turn, all of the guilds and corporations of Stamboul; tradesmen, artisans, merchants, labourers, civil servants, scholars, physicians, poets, musicians, entertainers, and functionaries of the religious, civil and military hierarchies of the Empire, all making a display before the Sultan and his court. And Evliya Efendi was there to describe them all in the most minute detail, including even the meanest and most insignificant of the guilds, omitting not even the lowly Gravediggers. 'Five hundred Gravediggers pass with shovels and hoes in their hands, asking the spectators where they shall dig their graves, and set up in this way a warning for many. The Gravediggers acknowledge as their patron Cain, the son of Adam, who murdered his brother Abel for a girl's sake. Not knowing how to hide the body, he saw a raven excavating with his beak a cocoa nut, in imitation of which he dug a grave to bury Abel's corpse. He is buried on Mount Ararat, in the place where Adam's kitchen stood. From that day Cain has remained the patron of all of those who shed blood and dig graves, as well as of the jealous.'

Even the poor madmen of the city were given an outing on this festive day, and Evliya describes their antics as they pass in the train of the Head Physician: 'Three hundred keepers of the bedlams of Constantinople pass in the procession, leading several hundred madmen in gold and silver chains. Some of the keepers carry bottles in their hands from which they give medicines to the madmen, while others beat or box the fools to keep them in order. Some of them are naked, some cry, some laugh, some swear and attack their keepers, which puts the spectators to flight. If I were to describe all the fits of the madmen and fools on such a day of public procession, I should fill a book.'

Also represented in the procession were the Corporation of Beggars, numbering, according to Evliya, seven thousand with their Sheikh. 'Relying on the text of the Koran: "Alms for the poor and wretched," they pass in a great crowd of strange figures dressed in woollen cloth and turbans of palm-leaves, crying "*Ya fettah!*" (O All-Merciful), some blind, some lame, some having lost a hand or foot, some naked and barefoot, and some mounted on asses. They place their Sheikh in the

A shop on the Street of the Scale-Makers

centre, and after his prayer is performed they all cry together "Allah, Allah, Amen!" and the sound of this cry of seven thousand tongues rends the sky. This prayer is performed for the Emperor's health immediately under the Alay Köşkü, where they receive alms.'

Besides the reputable merchants, tradesmen, artisans and craftsmen of the city, the procession included less savoury groups, such as, as Evliya tells us: 'The Corporation of Thieves and Footpads might be here noted as a very numerous one, who have an eye to our purses; but far be they from us. We say the same of the Corporation of Pimps and Bankrupts, who are innumerable. These thieves pay tribute to the two chief officers of the police, and get their subsistence by mingling in the crowds of Constantinople and by cheating foreigners.'

The next-to-last section in the procession was made up of the Fools and Mimics of Constantinople. According to Evliya: 'Whenever there is a feast of imperial circumcision, nuptials, or victory, from two to three hundred singers, comics, mimics and mischievous boys of the town, who have exhausted seventy cups of the poison of life and misrule, crowd together and play, day and night. They are divided into twelve companies.' The first of these companies were made up of young Gypsies and the last was composed of Jewish boys, and the two groups took turn in poking fun at one another as they marched along in the parade.

The twelfth company are two hundred Jewish boys, all tumblers, jugglers, fire-eaters, ball-players, and cup-bearers, who pass the whole night in showing their tricks, and ask more than one hundred piastres for a night's performance. As these Jewish boys have the greatest antipathy to the Gypsies, who compose the first company, they generally set a band of these Jewish boys against a band of Gypsies, which produces the strangest scenes. Thus, they represent the play of a Jew surprised *in flagrante* with a Gypsy girl; the girl is seated on an ass and conducted through the street with nasty intestines on her head, which makes the people nearly die with laughing. In short these twelve companies of boys vie with each other in producing the most voluptuous dances and the most comical scenes. They are all dressed in gold stuff, and endeavour to excel while passing under the Alay Köşkü, where the Emperor is seated, so as to attract his attention with their fits and tricks. Since Adam descended from Paradise on earth, never was there seen such a crowd of tempting boys as under Sultan Murat IV.

The last guild in the procession was that of the Tavern-Keepers. Evliya tells us that in Istanbul there were 'one thousand such places of misrule, kept by Greeks, Armenians and Jews. In the procession wine is not produced openly, and the Tavern-Keepers pass all in disguise and clad in armour. The boys of the taverns, all shameless drunkards, and all the partisans of wine pass singing songs, tumbling down and rising again.' The last of all to pass were the Jewish tavern-keepers, 'all masked and wearing the most precious dresses bedecked with jewels, carrying in their hands crystal and porcelain cups, out of which they pour sherbet instead of wine for the spectators.'

And so finally this fabulous parade came to an end as the last of the marchers passed the Alay Köşkü, 'after which the guilds accompanied their officers to their lodgings and everyone returned home'. Evliya then ends his account by saying that 'the procession of the imperial camp began its march at dawn and continued the whole day until sunset. On account of this parade all work and trade in Constantinople were stopped for three days, during which the riot and confusion filled the town to such a degree which is not to be expressed by language, and which I, the humble Evliya, only dared to describe. Nowhere else has such a procession been seen or shall be seen; it could only be carried into effect by the imperial orders of Sultan Murat IV.' And then Evliya, obviously exhausted by his long description of the imperial procession, concludes with this remark: 'Amen! By the Lord of all the Prophets; God be praised that I have overcome the task of describing the guilds and corporations of Constantinople!'

Yaşar Kasım and his pelican

5

The Galata Bridge

Nowhere else in town is the connection between the old Stamboul and the new more evident than on and around the Galata Bridge. Watching the colourful multitudes passing across the Golden Horn each day, we are sometimes inclined to think that we are back in Evliya's town, watching a somewhat disorderly procession of the guilds and corporations of the city, for many of the types that Evliya describes are still to be seen there today.

One of the best places from which to view the Galata Bridge is on the Stamboul shore of the Golden Horn, on the quay which is called the Fishermen's Meeting-Place. We often amuse ourselves there by boarding the floating Sea-Museum of Yaşar Kasım, where two senile seals splash and grunt in a pool of filth, delighting the peasants who pay one copper coin to watch. Yaşar Kasım is a foul-tempered dwarf. His advertisement is a lecherous-looking pelican with bloodshot eyes who stands balanced on one leg and looks cynically upon the passing scene.

But perhaps the pelican's eyes are jaundiced only by the boredom of his job, for we ourselves are always fascinated by the picturesque and lively activity on and around the bridge. Rattling trucks and buses and antique public taxis roar out of the narrow, crowded streets of Stamboul and put to rout their natural enemies, the police. They pass the city's single traffic light, ignoring its changing colours, and race madly across the bridge, enjoying their brief freedom before entering the narrow, crowded streets of Galata. Fleets of ferries honk and smoke and whistle obscenely upon their noisy arrivals and departures beside and under the bridge, like swift white and yellow water-bugs skimming to and from the maritime quarters of the town. The opposing crowds swarm on and off like two commuting armies colliding in a desperate amphibious struggle. A tourist caught between the lines finds himself teetering on the tilting gangway, slipping on the oily deck, tangling in the mooring ropes, tripping over the coal pile, and is finally sat upon by two voluminous ladies in the second-class lounge. A porter carrying a dozen empty oil-drums is locked in combat with a patriarch dragging home a sacrificial ram for the holidays. A legless beggar is trampled on by a giant blind man. A perfumed aristocrat is wrapped in reluctant embrace with a ragged farmer reeking of the sheepfold. An old woman struggles with an obstinate goat and is knocked down by a tree which is being carried aboard by a drunken forester. A hairy stoker, peering out from the flaming boiler-room, smiles with affection at a passing fisherman . . . The departing ferries leave the dock before the crowd is safely aboard, and there is a half-minute of great excitement as athletic young men leap across the widening gap. But the last one aboard is a crippled old crone who comes hobbling down the dock frantically waving her crooked cane. At the last possible moment she is thrown on to the ferry like a bag of old clothes. Unruffled, she picks herself up and engages in con-versation another bag of old clothes, her dear friend. The passengers then doze off while the ferry transports them to an older and more serene continent.

The Galata Bridge has a greater intimacy with the water it crosses than do most others in the world. As in human affairs, this intimacy can be the source of both pleasure and pain. The faint-hearted who are unwilling to risk such a hazardous intersection of the terrestrial and maritime life of this turbulent city should cross bridges suspended between two boroughs of a modern and well-ordered metropolis. Silver mackerel in red wooden tubs are hawked from skiffs at the foot of the bridge, and squatting entrepreneurs with a hook and a line and a flame sell fried-fish sandwiches and add one more smell to the city's garments. Bright orange and yellow caiques carrying fruits and vegetables sail under the bridge and in their passing graze foul black barges freighted with who knows what horror.

On the upper level of the bridge, nations of pedestrians pass in picturesque disarray. We had once the extravagant notion that these crowds were made up of two entirely independent mobs, one heading for a riot and the other escaping from the same disturbance, and that they had somehow gotten hopelessly entangled with one another. Young yokels stride bow-legged in tight-fitting Anatolian jodhpurs, their suits a patchwork mosaic of worn and faded fabrics, their squeaking oaken shoes thudding upon the pavement. Older men, resisting republican clothing-reform, are garbed in ancient, robe-like army overcoats or in cocoons of rags, wearing the vestigial tatters of old turbans on their grizzled heads. Their veiled and baggy-trousered women trail behind, surrounded by bedraggled children with running noses, carrying all their belongings rolled into enormous rug-wound bundles. These villagers, straight off the bus from eastern Anatolia, stare incredulously at the effete Stamboullus, with their lounge suits and fedoras, and their bare-armed, plume-haired and balloon-breasted wives. The Stamboullus, self-conscious of their own superiority, step nimbly through the unruly throng, seeking only to avoid contact with their uncouth country-cousins. They fail, inevitably, for it is impossible to cross the bridge without being bumped, struck, shoved aside, stomped and trampled on by sturdy peasants. You dodge to escape impalement by a porter transporting a sheaf of steel spikes, try to pass between two other porters only to find that they are carrying between them a large pane of glass, narrowly escape death under the wheels of a tumbril stacked high with coffins, and are finally struck down by a Fairbanks weighing-scale with which a young man hopes to make his fortune in Stamboul, a penny at a time.

One thus learns not to rush across the bridge, but to stand aside and watch the passing crowd, for it is safer and more amusing. Observe that crowd of ruddy-faced rustics, as they stand in awe listening to a fast-talking huckster extolling the merits of cardboard sandals for the barefooted, alchemical folk-medicines for the incurably ill, plastic raincoats for the ragged, and leaking fountain-pens for the illiterate. These pedlars have the sound and mobility and weather sense of a flock of magpies; scurrying after a group of gullible peasants here, fleeing from the market police there, producing umbrellas for sale when clouds threaten and sunglasses when it clears. They are there with hooks and lines to sell when fish are running, and when we see them hawking stovepipes we know that winter is near.

From the safety of our bridge-side reviewing stand we can also observe the porters as they pass, sparing ourselves the peril of being run down by them. These porters, or *hamals* as they are called, carry much of the city's trade and commerce on their strong backs, for they can transport their loads through steep and narrow alleys where carts and trucks could never pass. These underpaid atlases stagger across the bridge bearing burdens truly herculean; baskets piled high with black mountains of coal; bristling thickets of kindling wood; whole bakeries of stacked bread loaves; entire factories of machine parts; crowded roomfuls of furniture, including refrigerators and grand pianos. With the help of ten of these *hamals* one could sack a fair-sized town. In the old days, it is said, they carried sick persons to the hospital on their backs, and transported drunken revellers to their homes from the taverns of Galata. A generation ago the Armenian *hamals* used to celebrate the end of their long and gruelling year with a drunken spree, at the climax of which a crowd of them staggered down the streets of Galata with poles on their shoulders, supporting on strings between them – a single egg. They still shuffle along patiently, bent double under their brutal burdens, experts on the cobblestones of this town.

When we grow tired of watching this daily riot, we join other strollers as they head for the cafés and teahouses under the bridge, waiting for evening. We sit with them there, sipping tea or rakı or puffing dreamily on a nargile, and notice how the late afternoon sun tints the Golden Horn in soft pastels, giving its filthy waters a brief and spurious beauty. This is the best place from which to view Stamboul and to take pleasure in its pale colours.

We first noticed how pale the colours of the city were when a pedlar appeared on the bridge one winter day with beach-balls for sale. Istanbul is so full of insane anachronisms and eccentric contrasts that the sight of beach-balls being sold in the middle of winter did not in itself seem strange. (Would you believe balloons being hawked in a snowstorm or kites in a hurricane?) It was just that the iridescent sectors of the balls – psychedelic yellows, reds and greens – gave an electric shock to eyes used to the city's browns and duns and greys. When the pedlar passed we saw that there was not a bright colour in sight. Age and dirt and the vaporous climate had taken the flash from all colours and the sharpness from all outlines, leaving not a straight line nor a primary colour in town. For this reason the old wooden houses of Stamboul, the venerable *ahşap evleri*, have become veritable palettes of pale colours. An old wooden house will weather, crack, fade and totter in a manner which depends on where it stands, what winds blow upon it, and the habits and vitality of its inhabitants. Thus its walls can become as brown and wrinkled in as many ways as can an old man's face. The *ahşap evleri* lean against one another like ranks of old pensioners puffing aluminium pipes, and their smoke crowns the city in pale pink clouds.

With the beginning of the autumnal rains the sun is gone until spring and we are left with only the palest and most indigenous of the city's colours. In the diffuse winter light which casts no shadows wet cobbles shine in the rain and the lead domes of mosques are brighter than swords. Seen from the Galata Bridge, Stamboul seems a grey ruin worn down by freezing rain and the Golden Horn becomes a polluted moat filled with the bloated corpses of the city's past. But when all hope seems gone and we are about to surrender to our annual midwinter gloom, we are briefly cheered by the amber glow from a teahouse door, or by the sight of lamplight refracted in the stained-glass windows of an old mosque. And as we stroll across the bridge under the arctic light of a winter moon we observe that the grey old city is indeed imperial.

The imperial quality of the city is sensed the first time one crosses the Galata Bridge to Stamboul. Nearly all of the imperial Osmanli mosques can then be seen standing proudly on the ridge above the Golden Horn, their domes and minarets silhouetted against the western sky. The imperial mosque most familiar to ordinary citizens is Yeni Cami, the New Mosque, which presides like a queen over the Stamboul end of the Galata Bridge. Although the New Mosque was built in the first half of the seventeenth century her years wear well upon her. Her walls and domes and minarets are blackened by the smoke of ferry boats, she is assailed by all the foul weather that howls down the Bosphorus from the Black Sea in winter, and her peace is disturbed by the roar of the traffic and the clamour of the markets which surround her. She seems to share the life of the city in a way that no other imperial mosque quite does, and at no loss to her dignity. When we slosh across the bridge on a stormy day, water dripping from our beards, we see the mosque dripping too, pigeons and sea-birds huddled around her domes, miserable beggars seeking shelter under her arcades, exhausted pedlars from the local markets limping towards her in fatigue. Inside, the faithful find shelter and peace, their worn feet comforted by soft rugs and carpets, their eyes resting themselves on the harmonious forms of the interior, their minds eased by the echoing sounds of repeated prayers. Then, when good weather returns, Yeni Cami is the first to celebrate, catching the sun on her granite walls and lead domes and brightening the quarter over which she rules. And on the holy nights of the Islamic year hundreds of lights are strung from her slender minarets and her façade is illuminated by brilliant floodlamps, looming like a cascade of light on the dark Stamboul shore of the Golden Horn. It is no wonder that her beggars and pedlars will practise at no other mosque in town.

And when the beggars and pedlars have finished their day they usually go to eat at one of the humble cook-shops in the shadow of Yeni Cami. Some of these are located aboard the flotilla of caiques which are anchored beside the bridge, looking like the medieval galleons of a mad admiral who ran his fleet aground while enamoured of the pale colours and heady odours of the Stamboul shore. One of these sinking caravels is the People's Sea-Restaurant, which we are sure is the wreck of the Argo. And beside the Argo there is a floating tavern called the Workers' Cultural Club, much frequented by the local fishmongers and *hamals*. We often pause here at twilight, if we have spent a day in the vicinity of the Galata Bridge, and have a rakı or two before boarding our ferry for home. From here we can look out along the Golden Horn, now gilded by the last colours of the fallen sun, and see the lights of evening coming on across the way in the sinful streets of Galata. As night falls the traffic on the bridge begins to dwindle, and soon the square before Yeni Cami is as quiet and serene as the interior of the mosque itself. We then pay for our drinks and depart, pausing on the bridge for a few moments before descending to the landing-stage. We see that there are now only a few last stragglers upon the bridge, mostly old men and women limping slowly homeward from the markets. Across the roadway, in the Fishermen's Meeting Place, Yaşar Kasım has just closed and locked his Sea-Museum and is now waddling across the bridge to his hovel in the slums of Galata, his pelican perched on one leg upon his shoulder. When he has gone the Galata Bridge is quite deserted, except for a few lonely exiles reluctant to go home. Standing there and watching the end of this daily parade of life across the Galata Bridge, we are reminded of the words which Evliya Efendi wrote three centuries ago, as he watched the last of the imperial procession pass by: 'Such is the crowd and population of that great capital, Stamboul, which may God guard from all celestial and earthly mischief till the end of the World. Amen!'

6

Eminönü

Eminönü, the quarter around the Stamboul end of the Galata Bridge, was in Evliya's time and is still today the principal market area of the city. Many of the guilds which he describes in the imperial procession of Murat IV had their headquarters there in just the same places then as they do today. Were it not for the distraction of motorised traffic and the disguise of modern clothing, Evliya would probably still recognise this quarter and its inhabitants. For this was the neighbourhood in which he was born and spent his youth and early manhood, and these are many of the same people whom he describes in the procession of the guilds.

Pride of place among the guilds in this quarter must be given to the fishmongers, whose colourful and rambunctious market occupies the area just upstream from the Galata Bridge. It was located there in Evliya's day, and for many centuries before, for even in Byzantine times the local entry way through the sea-walls in this quarter was known as the Fish-Market Gate. As Evliya writes in the *Seyahatname*: 'The establishment of the Fishermen is outside the Flour-Hall, at the old fish-market on the Golden Horn.' And Evliya gives this description of the guild of the Fishermen as it passes in the imperial procession: 'The Fishermen adorn their shops on litters with many thousand fish, among which many monsters of the ocean are to be seen. They exhibit dolphins on chains, sea-horses, walruses, whales, and other kinds of fish of great size, which they catch a couple of days before the procession and load wagons with them drawn by seventy-eight buffaloes. They pass, crying "Hi!" and "Ho!", to the great amazement of the beholders. The enfranchised fishermen also collect various insects of the sea, and a

Galata Bridge, with Yeni Cami in the background

great number of them carry in their hands halberds, harpoons, muskets
and artificial trees.'

And for the impatient fish-addicts who cannot bear any delay in
devouring their purchases, there are a number of fish-cooks stationed
just beside the market. Their establishments are quite modest, just a
chair and table or two wedged in among the stalls of the fishmongers,
whose customers they engulf in smoke whenever they stoke their grills
to fry a fish. But don't turn up your nose at them, for these fish-cooks
were feeding the citizens of this town centuries before the first modern
restaurant ever opened here. Here is Evliya's description of the guild of
the fish-cooks as they pass in the procession, following immediately
after the fishmongers: 'The Fish-Cooks are all infidel Greeks who cook
fish in different ways, some with olive oil and some with linseed oil; they
also cook mussel-pilaf, oysters and a soup of *kefal* fish. They also have
oysters called *lakoz* which are very strengthening. If eaten quickly they
taste like a green slime, but they are very envigorating, and are therefore
wholesome to men who wish to please their wives; in short it is a delicacy
for debauchees . . . In the public procession the Fish-Cooks pass singing
songs and making jests. They are a comical set of fellows and made the
Emperor laugh much, who was of a very merry disposition.'

The largest fruit and vegetable market in the city is also located in
the neighbourhood of Yeni Cami, fighting there for space and custom
with the adjacent fish-market. The produce in this market is generally
fresher and cheaper than elsewhere in town, making it almost worth
the perils of shopping there, enduring the bruises suffered by you and
your purchases, the deafening noise and the constant danger of being
trampled to death in the swirling stew of mud and burst fruit and
mangled vegetables underfoot. All of the vendors in this market were
represented in the imperial procession, behaving there in much
the same manner as they do today. Here, for example, is Evliya's
description of the guild of Fruit-Merchants:

They pass on wagons adorned with all kinds of fruits. They also make
artificial trees of apples, apricots and other kinds of fruit, each carried

on poles by eight or ten men. Others make kiosks with fountains playing, the four sides of which are festooned with fruit. Their boys, who are seated in these kiosks, bargain with the spectators and throw fruit to them. Some dress in robes made of chestnuts, reciting verses of the Koran while holding rosaries of dried raisins. They also build artificial ships, which are full of fruit, each ship being towed by a thousand men. The sails, masts, prow and stern of each of these ships are ornamented with fruit kernels. Merchants flock in crowds to enter these fruit-ships to fill their baskets. With the greatest noise and quarrelling arising from these simulated sales, they pass the Alay Köşkü. This is a faithful representation of what occurs at the port on the arrival of every fruit-ship, where such noise arises, and many heads are broken without the injured persons being allowed to ask for legal satisfaction.

The most distinguished of all the markets which cluster around Yeni Cami is the Mısır Çarşısı, or the Egyptian Market, perhaps better known as the Spice Bazaar. The Spice Bazaar is a veritable museum of eastern smells; drugs, gums, herbs, spices, perfumes and incense, as if all the aromatic lands of Asia had concentrated their most exotic odours here under one roof so as to introduce the traveller to the heady atmosphere of the Orient. As Evliya writes: 'The Egyptian Grocers pass armed on wagons filled with baskets of ginger, pepper, cardamum, cinamum, cloves, rhubarb, spikenard and aloes, forming altogether three thousand items.' The Bazaar is also famous for its coffee stores, where, according to Evliya, 'The Coffee-Merchants are employed in grinding coffee for all of Constantinople.' The Bazaar also houses some of the best shops in town for buying *pastırma*, the delicious dried beef which for centuries has been a favourite Stamboul dish. Here is Evliya's description of this guild as it passes in the procession: 'The Merchants of Pastırma are Moslems and are called the people of Manavgatoğlu. This man was once eating excrement in a golden dish at a royal circumcision and said to the Emperor: "Glorious monarch, naught remains!" meaning that there was no more excrement left. Since then the boys of the town always run after these people, crying, "Naught remains!" In the procession some of these people wear the hides of oxen and bulls, wearing the horns and tails on their heads. Some take sheep heads and feet and make a complete dress from head to foot of dried beef, carrying hams instead of clubs, and with banners, boots, trousers and saddles all of dried beef, and pass in the procession repeating the words of their patron Manavgatoğlu, "Naught remains!" They are a strange and comical set of people.'

The principal flower-market of the city is located just behind Yeni Cami, adding its perfumed scents to the aromas of the Spice Bazaar and the more earthy smells of the fish-market. Evliya gives this brief description of these merchants as they pass in the procession: 'At the shops of these Flower-Merchants at all seasons of the year are found dishes full of fruits and flowers, which are offered as presents to the vezirs and great men. They make a great show in the procession, being an exquisitely armed troop. They carry on poles a number of kiosks, wherein fine boys reclining on golden cushions do service.'

On the northern side of this be-flowered square behind Yeni Cami we find the bird-market. Your true Stamboullu is as addicted to the song of birds as he is to flowers, and it is a rare teahouse or barber shop that has not its warbling captive in an ornate cage. And as any Stamboullu knows, the most beautiful bird-song is that of the nightingale, who serenades us along the hills and valleys of the Bosphorus in April and May. Evliya tells us that in his day there were five hundred Nightingale-Merchants in Stamboul, and describes them thus as they pass in the imperial procession: 'They furnish great men and barber shops with nightingales, which by their melodies enrapture the soul. They have some most precious cages set with onyxes and pearls; some of these cages are worth a thousand piastres and are only given as presents to kings. In these cages the nightingales, excited by the noise of the crowd, sing loudly and merrily, vying with each other in their warbling notes. In other cages talking parrots and chattering parakeets are seen, some of which recite the Sura Ikhlass and other prayers.'

But many Stamboullus feel that it is cruel to cage a bird, particularly a nightingale, a sentiment with which Evliya evidently agreed. For he tells us that: 'Our fathers had a proverb, saying, "Who kills a bird-merchant or a gambler may be called a *gazi* (a warrior for the faith)." The Bird-Merchants are an abject sort of people.'

The steps of Yeni Cami and the great square before it are always crowded with itinerant pedlars, hawking their poor wares above the noise and tumult of the crowds and traffic. The most popular of these are the *saka*, or water-sellers, who will give you a cool glass of spring water for twenty-five *kuruş*. The *saka*, who are the most picturesquely attired vendors in town, are still outfitted in much the same fashion as they were when Evliya saw them passing in the imperial procession: 'The Water-Carriers are all on foot, dressed in black leather jackets, carrying canisters on their backs. Various ornaments of flowers are stuck on their heads, and in their hands they carry cups of crystal and china, the interiors of which are shining with onyxes, jaspers, turquoises or gold, out of which they give drink to the Moslems. They do this in remembrance of the martyrs of Kerbala, saying that they shall drink to the health of Hasan and Hüseyin. Some recite verses composed in the same vein, and others quote the verse of the Koran: "We have given to thee water from the Spring of Paradise." '

And if the *saka*'s cup is not made of crystal or china but of tin, and if he grunts at you instead of reciting effusive verses from the Koran, pay no heed, for his water is probably just as cool and refreshing as it was in Evliya's day.

After a few hours of shopping in Eminönü, one might feel inclined to restore oneself with food and drink. The area around Yeni Cami abounds with cheap and modest little cook-shops, where the proletariat fortify themselves before resuming their work or shopping. Evliya called the men who run such places Cooks of the Poor, and describes them thus as they pass in the procession: 'The Cooks of the Poor pass, all well-dressed, with stoves built on wagons, and shops finely laid out with precious china plates and dishes, with tankards and basins, towels and fans of peacock feathers which are moved by servants while the cooks are preparing dinners. If some hungry guest enters their shop they cry

out, "Look, a greasy guest!" and then name their dishes in a rhyming
strain. At every cook's shop there is found at least one carver, who after
having set the dish before the guest, saying *"Bismillah"* (In God's name),
eats two morsels and then bids the guest eat. This is the custom of the
cook-shops at Constantinople, which is practised nowhere else.'

But old Stamboullus who have worked in this quarter for years
generally prefer a somewhat more secluded restaurant, where they can
be free for a time from the hurly-burly of the markets. This is Pandelis,
a little fish-restaurant which stands just across the street from Ahi Çelebi
Camii, the mosque where Evliya had his vision of the Prophet. Pandelis
is one of the oldest restaurants in Stamboul and still one of the very best,
as evidenced by the sight of the well-fed and well-preserved gaffers who
dine there daily. Within, the street noises are muted and one is revived
by a bowl of hot fish-soup and a half bottle of cold rakı, a combination
that has been known to evoke visions less spiritual than that of Evliya
Efendi, but just as satisfying. Gazing contentedly through Pandelis' dirty
windows after our meal, we see that the late afternoon sun has mellowed
the scene outside and given a golden glow to the clouds of street-dust
swirling in the wake of passing wagons. Mellowed ourselves, we decide
once again that this broken-down old town is still beautiful. The *hamals*
outside are not given to such romantic thoughts, for they are still
staggering down the street under their crushing burdens, choking on the
dust which to us looks golden. If they could think they would declare
the town a living hell; but they cannot, and thereby achieve a kind of
brutal salvation. But we are not often aware of this in Pandelis.

We usually leave Pandelis when the sun has dropped behind the
mosques above the Golden Horn, and seek our various pleasures around
the town. This is the magic hour in Stamboul. Ramshackle folk-buses
and public taxis rattle down the avenues like old street-dogs, never quite
pointed straight ahead. The men of Stamboul are headed home, if they
have one, from their work or from their idleness. Teahouses resound
with the slap of playing-cards, the click of *tavla*-counters, and the debates
of unshaven and unelected parliaments. Fruit sellers polish shining
galleries of apples, hang chandeliers of bananas, weave tapestries of

Corn sellers dozing by the steps of Yeni Cami

onions and garlic, construct black pyramids of olives. Fishmongers
sprinkle glistening tubs of mackerel, red mullet, swordfish and tuna,
artistically arranging glittering fins and gaping mouths so as to seduce
the passing piscivore. Embassies of expectant waiters stand in restaurant
doorways, pointing to tempting displays of skewered kebabs, quivering
puddings, globular sweets, and mounds of belly-swelling pilaf. Barber-
shops are illuminated like little theatres in which half the men in town
are being shaved and perfumed by the other half, themselves unshaven
and unperfumed. The framed inscription on the barber's wall announces
that the shop is under the protection of Selman, barber to the Prophet,
of whom it was said that 'Paradise longs for Selman every day, and every
night three times.' In the street, itinerant sellers of water, *ayran*, and *boza*
minister to the thirst of the milling crowds, and street-hawkers rally to
sell one last useless item to pay for their suppers. Hopeful children crowd
round the travelling fortune-teller and his divinatory bird. Young girls
rattle with their buckets to the street fountain and housewives haul up
the evening's groceries to their tenement windows with line and basket.
Kerchiefed crones call after their fleeing grandchildren, while their old
husbands mark the weekly football-pool in the light of the street lamps
which shine outside their windows. From every house and shop Istanbul
Radio blares and the street hums with the melancholy music of the saz.
Street vendors fill the night air with the enticing smells of hot corn and
roasting chestnuts and bakeries incense the neighbourhood with the
sacramental odour of hot bread.

Seated by a teahouse window, in the Street of the Giant's Son, we
watch the evening crowds as they begin to drift homeward; fresh-faced
peasants dressed in their village finery; brilliantly costumed nomad
women wearing necklaces of golden coins; lunar-featured Kurdish
soldiers walking together in pairs, delicately holding hands; exhausted
hamals, relieved of their burdens, staggering towards their brutal
pleasures in the slums; tired Anatolian workers ritually bringing home
the family bread; shy clusters of veiled Macedonian women in black
robes; bent old Armenians with sorrowful faces; blue-eyed and marble-
pale Greek widows with Hellenic profiles; leather-skinned and

barnacle-handed Laz fishermen; Sephardic Jews with Old Testament faces by El Greco; medusa-headed Gypsy girls queening it over the cobbles; snow-bearded ancients returning from the mosque like figures in a Biblical procession . . .

Soon the crowd has dwindled to a few stragglers and the market streets grow gradually quiet. Fruit sellers put away their produce with the same care with which they arranged it twelve long hours before, now and then looking down the road, as if hoping for one last apple-lover to appear. The fish-market closes and cats descend to scavenge the cobbles. One-by-one metal shop-fronts come clanging down along the market streets, and watchmen's whistles answer one another around the darkening quarter. Off in the distance we can hear the cracked voice of an old *boza*-pedlar as he proclaims to the empty streets that his *boza* is exceptionally fine . . . It was an evening that Evliya Efendi would have recognised and cherished, in his old neighbourhood by the Golden Horn.

Mahmutpaşa Market, selling new and used clothing

7

The Avenue of the Long Market

The quarter of the town occupying the slope of the hill above Yeni Cami is generally known as Uzun Çarşı. The district takes its name from Uzun Çarşı Caddesi, the Avenue of the Long Market, which leads uphill from the Golden Horn towards Beyazıt Square. This is indeed an appropriate name, for this narrow street (avenue it is not) is one long continuous market, lined with shops, stalls and barrows, in which merchants and vendors hawk all the world's cheap and shoddy wares. Would you like a tin suitcase made of pressed American beer-cans, a deafening Mickey Mouse alarm clock from Red China, a machine-gun-shooting mechanical man from Germany, an enormous pair of felt-padded Bulgarian brassieres looking like a brace of coolie sun-hats, a nifty pair of Anatolian jodhpurs just right for an evening in an Erzurum teahouse, and a horse-blanket to keep your wife warm while she waits for you in your unheated hovel? Or would you prefer a sweater that scratches the neck like steel wool, shirts made for a chicken-breasted hunchback, a chequered jacket suitable for a racetrack tout, socks that shrink to a frizzled tangle of itching threads, pointed patent-leather shoes with backs already folded down for easy removal in mosques; and for your wife, a black *çarşaf* to cover her face, a shroud-like overcoat to disguise her shape, and baggy *şalvar* so voluminous that no man will ever be tempted to look upon her? These things are all to be found in the Avenue of the Long Market, and they are all bargains.

Uzun Çarşı is also one of the principal industrial districts of Stamboul, a city innocent of zoning laws and contemptuous of town-planning. There are factories, forges, machine-shops, textile mills, chemical plants, tinsmiths, carpentry shops and printing-presses, most of them housed in the dark and unhealthy chambers of old Ottoman hans, employing machines and techniques unchanged since the Industrial Revolution, worked by soot-blackened young boys who never heard of child-labour laws and by toil-broken older men unacquainted with even the most elemental rights of labour. But, undaunted, they pound and bang and saw away from dawn till past sunset, just as their predecessors have there for generations past. Here, then, is Evliya's description of some of the more colourful of the industrial guilds in the imperial procession:

The troops of the Tinmen pass with all kinds of tools for bending, cleansing and stretching. They put in the middle of the road a large trunk, on which from 14 to 16 men hammering with all their might show the excellency of their art. The seniors of this guild have beards of different colours from the effect of the damp of brass, some green, some sulphur-coloured . . . The Saw-Makers are 200 men, with 80 shops. Their first patron was Ismail, a Jew, who invented the saw at Aleppo in order to saw Zaccharias in half . . . The Aquafortis-Makers are 100 men, with 22 factories; they are for the most part Jews. The inventor of aquafortis was Solomon, who collected the water dripping from leprous Dives. It is so sharp a substance that its vapour alone tinges the feathers of birds, and the Jews who manage it become coloured green, yellow and red, and their nails are blackened. In India they dye their teeth with this aquafortis, and you find men who have teeth of 32 different colours in their mouth. This accursed aquafortis is also a requisite of alchemy and the Jews are devoted to the study of that subject. They pass in the procession on litters burning aquafortis from sulphur-water and sulphur-oil.

The most picturesque of the old Ottoman buildings in which these industrial guilds are housed is the Valide Han, which stands just off Uzun Çarşı Caddesi near its upper end. This han was built early in the seventeenth century by the Sultan Valide Kösem, mother of Murat IV and Crazy İbrahim. Evliya tells us that it 'was originally the palace of Cerrah Mehmet Paşa, but having fallen into decay it was rebuilt by the Valide. This han and that of Mahmut Paşa are the largest in

Constantinople and its stables are capable of holding one thousand horses and mules.'

Although the Valide Han is still grand and impressive, it is badly battered and bears the scars of its long and active commercial career. At first sight it has the appearance of a walled medieval town in a state of siege. The vast interior courtyard is crowded with ramshackle houses; a tottering line of them stagger around the periphery of the courtyard, leaning against the walls of the han for support. Others, designed by acrobatic folk-architects, have been constructed up under the vaults of the arcades on the upper floors, and a perilous few even perch on the roof of the han or hang like bird cages above the main gate. They are wedged and propped and squeezed into every improbable corner, defying the laws of nature as well as those of the municipality. The interior chambers of the han are given over to every conceivable form of industry and commerce, of which the principal products appear to be noise, odour, and the insanely colourful. In the rear courtyard there is a textile factory, perhaps the most self-contained in existence, where bleating sheep are driven in at one end and finished fabrics emerge packaged at the other. Elsewhere there are clattering printing-presses and looms and machine-shops staffed by sweating men and boys who shout to make themselves heard above the din. An old Armenian invites one into a vault filled with spices and lights an incensed candle to exhibit his aromatic wares, while across the passageway a circle of Gypsy women pause in their weaving of funeral bouquets to shout obscenities at passers-by. Strolling pedlars hawk their wares among the struggling crowds of merchants, drivers, *hamals* and horse-drawn wagons. In a courtyard café, an itinerant barber shaves a lawyer who is negotiating a contract with a rug-merchant leaning from a balcony on the floor above. Under the vine-draped arcade merchants are gathered around glowing *mangals*, and from their hand-gestures one can tell that they are talking of trade in the old-fashioned oriental manner, just as they probably did here in Evliya's day.

Hard by the back gate of the Valide Han one finds the principal second-hand clothing market of the city, where the poor of Stamboul and its thieves trade one another old and tattered garments. It is said that you can stroll through this market, if you are clever enough, sell all the clothes you are wearing, and later buy them back farther down the Avenue of the Long Market, still returning home with a small profit in your pocket. Your clothes, however, will never again smell the same.

At the upper end of this thieves' bazaar we find the city's largest market of second-hand shoes. (And if you wonder who on earth would buy shoes second-hand, well, just stroll any weekday down the Avenue of the Long Market.) Evliya tells us that in his time there were two hundred merchants of old shoes who had their shops in this area. They marched in the procession along with the Shoe-Merchants and Shoemakers, the latter of which was one of the most powerful guilds in the city. Evliya describes them thus as they parade before the Alay Köşkü: 'The Shoemakers pass all armed, but barefoot and bareheaded, adorning their shops with all kinds of shoes and slippers, of all possible dimensions, including boots of an enormous size, big enough to hold two men. The Shoe-Merchants hawk their wares according to an account which is known only among themselves, and the scheme of which is none other than to cheat the buyers, of which they boast. They are a merciless set of people, but every man stands in need of them. They are followed by the Old-Shoe Merchants, who adorn their shops with ancient shoes.'

And so they still do today, on the Avenue of the Long Market.

The markets for second-hand clothing and shoes spill over into the infamous Bit Pazarı, or Flea Market, which is located just beyond the upper end of Uzun Çarşı Caddesi, at the edge of Beyazıt Square. The Flea Market seems to have been situated in this spot in Evliya's time too, for he tells us that the Dung-Searchers and the Rag-and-Bone Pickers had their headquarters near the Coral Mosque, which still stands at the head of the Avenue of the Long Market. This is the maddest and most colourful of all the street-markets in Stamboul. Every great city has its flea-market, but perhaps the one here surpasses them all for the simple reason that most material objects are used far longer in Stamboul than elsewhere, because of the perpetual lack of new things to buy.

Nothing is ever thrown away, but is repaired or mended, passed on, traded, resold or stolen, perhaps acquiring a new identity as part of a composite of other cannibalised components, passing and re-passing through the Bit Pazarı, which thus acts as a kind of second-hand heart in the circulatory system of junk which is Stamboul.

The setting of the Bit Pazarı is a bit more bizarre than ever these days, since the municipality decided to dig a tunnel under Beyazıt Square, right through the centre of the Flea Market. The tunnel was for a period abandoned, half-finished, like so many other grandiose plans to improve this once-handsome square, and the merchants of the Bit Pazarı, like the human fleas they are, settled back into their old nests among the raw mounds of earth, the ditches filled with rainwater, the middens of garbage and the piles of cobblestones. To save their customers from falling into the abandoned tunnel, the flea-merchants constructed a barricade across the end of their street, a second-hand wall of broken bicycles, wrecked cars, ruined furniture and fragments of fallen buildings, all bound together with wire, tree-branches and stovepipe, those civic sinews of Stamboul. The scene in the Bit Pazarı is one of incredible noise and lunatic activity; three peasants laugh hysterically while they pound madly on a broken piano, a pedlar auctions off a lot of sprung and torn umbrellas and nearly impales an old man who had been sleeping on a red plush couch he had purchased an hour before, a Gypsy boy picks up a brass telescope from a pile of junk and discovers mountains on the daytime moon, a barefoot tramp stumbles about trying to sell one blade of a pair of scissors, two hideous farmers admire themselves in a gilt-framed rococo mirror, and a crowd of truant school-boys careen wildly around the market on wrecked bicycles with flat tyres and spokeless helical wheels, pursued by an irate flea-merchant, all to the music of a dozen gramophones blaring out incoherent tunes from warped records played on dying machines. A brief stroll through this junk-museum reveals: a pair of tennis rackets without strings, a box of eyeglass frames without lenses, framed photographs of obese Ottoman families, an illustrated advertisement for a depilatory cream showing a mustachioed lady before and after, companion busts of a

Teutonic Troll and a German Stormtrooper, a lens-less movie-projector filled with dead leaves, piles of cracked and bent phonograph records, an empty flit-can of Havana Flyspray, a box of watch-works, a carton of torn and deflated footballs, a broken clock with Arabic numerals but no hands (a symbol here?), a smashed globe of the world half-filled with garbage (another symbol?), a box of burned-out radio-tubes, a pair of deer antlers, a composite picture of the African tribes and another of the American Indian nations, two huge gilt-framed oil-paintings, one of Judith holding the dripping head of Holofernes and the other of Saul attempting to slay David (great for a whorehouse parlour), a watch which when wound sets its hands racing rapidly around the cracked face (time passes rapidly in the Bit Pazarı); in addition to a sordid assortment of such junk as: rusted locks without keys and keys without locks, bicycle seats, blown-out automobile tyres, unmatched pairs of sole-less shoes, the split halves of a plastic toilet-seat, bald shaving brushes, toothless combs, sprigs of plastic flowers, a step-on garbage-can filled with garbage, a rotted plastic turtle and a deflated rubber elephant. And this broken-down encyclopaedia can never be complete, for it is added to each hour in the Bit Pazarı by a procession of scavengers, junkmen, paupers and thieves, without whose contributions Stamboul's second-hand economy would cease to function.

On my most recent visit to the Bit Pazarı I was attracted by a crowd which had gathered at the end of the street. I walked over and found that three huge sailor's chests had been delivered to a flea-merchant there. The crowd waited expectantly and speculated upon the contents of these three trunks, for there seemed to be a certain air of mystery about them. The flea-merchant took advantage of the drama, hoping thus to increase his sales, and proceeded to open the first chest with very elaborate gestures. It proved to contain thousands of very used toothbrushes. I started to laugh but soon stopped when I saw how rapidly the old toothbrushes were selling; they were, I was told, in great demand among bootblacks, who use them to apply polish. The second chest proved to contain several thousand fountain-pens with smashed and shattered nibs. With my newly acquired respect for his commercial acuity, I theorised that this magpie merchant had obtained a large supply of nibs which he would fit into these pens, resell them as new and reap a neat profit; and that, surely, explained what the third chest contained. I forced my way through the crowd to be present at the moment when the chest was opened. When the rusted lock was finally sprung and the iron-bound lid forced back, I looked inside and found myself being stared at by a huge pile of disembodied dolls' eyes of all sizes and colours, unmatched and unaligned, together seeming like a cross-eyed audience viewed over the footlights of a madhouse theatre. At that point I decided to leave the Bit Pazarı for good, leaving unanswered the question of who in Stamboul purchases dolls' eyes and for what reason. But if you ever need a pair for an eyeless doll, you can surely find them for sale on the Avenue of the Long Market.

A shop owner in the Market of Second-hand Books

8

Beyazıt Square

If Stamboul can be said to have a centre, then it is probably Beyazıt Meydanı. Bordered on one side by the various institutions of Istanbul University and on the other by the Covered Bazaar, it is thus at the hub of the old city's active daily life. Time was, and not so very long ago, when this was one of the liveliest and most picturesque squares in the city, shaded by venerable trees and lined with teahouses, cafés and market stalls, filled with colourful throngs passing to and from the mosque, the markets and the university. But now a large part of the square has been cut through and paved over in the interest of the automobile, and only here and there can one find vestiges of its former charm. Nevertheless, it is still as lively as it ever was, if not as beautiful.

Beyazıt Meydanı, like most of the other great squares in Stamboul, centres upon an imperial mosque, in this case that of Sultan Beyazıt II. Completed in 1506, this is the oldest imperial mosque still standing in the city, and it has been the focal point of life in this part of Stamboul almost as long as this has been a Turkish town. From the description which Evliya gives of the mosque and its courtyard, it would seem that the scene is very much the same now as it was in his day: 'As this mosque was entirely built with lawful money, it has great spiritual advantages; and being situated in the centre of the markets of Istanbul, it is crowded day and night by thousands of devout Moslems, who are offering up their prayers there without ceasing. Round the outer and inner courts of this mosque there are shops of all kinds of trades, with a public kitchen, a refectory, a hostel for travellers, a school for instructing the poor and rich in the Koran and a college for lectures in the art of reciting it. The courtyard has six gates, and is adorned externally with lofty trees, under the shade of which some thousand of people gain a livelihood by selling various kinds of things.'

Many of the pious foundations of the Beyazıdiye which Evliya mentions are still serving the people of Stamboul in one way or another, and the courtyard is still filled with pedlars hawking their wares to the passing crowds. The mosque and its courtyard are a haven in this rough, noisy quarter, and *hamals* and street vendors find a brief peace here when their work allows them a few moments of freedom. The outer courtyard is always crowded with *hamals*, who sit along the walls with their harnesses still strapped to their backs, as if they were beasts of burden. They rest there quietly, puffing on fragments of cigarettes which they have gleaned from the cobbles, staring off into the distance and dreaming of God knows what paradise, putting off for as long as they can the moment when they must struggle to their feet and resume their labours. Other *hamals* have left their harnesses at the door of the mosque and are praying inside; long ranks and columns of barefoot, kneeling men, rocking back and forth in the ritual postures of Islamic prayer and pressing their foreheads humbly to the worn carpets, figures of touching dignity even in their rags. The street vendors pray here too, and the rear of the mosque is lined with the trays and portable cases in which they carry their wares around town. Looking into one of these trays and observing its pathetic contents, one wonders how it could provide a living for a man and his family – but it is all they have and they do their best. We once saw an old vendor of roasted chestnuts sitting in the courtyard and weeping after the police had broken his little grill and thrown his chestnuts to the ground because he had no licence. We helped him salvage what we could but he felt that it was hopeless, for without his grill he was finished. But he somehow managed to make another grill and was back again the next day selling his chestnuts. And so the street vendor prays quietly in the old mosque of Sultan Beyazıt, and then picks up his tray and goes out again into the courtyard to hawk his wares above the din of a hundred other pedlars, proclaiming that his stale chestnuts are the most delicious in Stamboul.

Apart from the five official occasions of public prayer, the faithful wander into Beyazıt Camii at all times of the day, from dawn until late evening, and there perform their private devotions. They are of all types and social classes, from well-dressed businessmen to ragged beggars, reflecting the traditional absence of class distinction in Islam. They enter gravely, shoes in hand, and walk barefoot across the carpets to their favourite spots in the mosque, beside a marble pillar, perhaps, or before a cool window looking out into the courtyard. In the side aisles young theology students sit cross-legged with the Koran held open before them on little wooden stands and read aloud, rapidly and mindlessly. In the rear galleries a harassed *hoca* leads groups of distracted little boys, trying to teach them how to read and recite the Koran. When the *hoca* leaves for a moment to catch a breath of air or to regain his sanity, the boys begin wrestling on the floor and playing tag around the columns. In a far corner of the mosque a sober group of white-bearded theologians discuss fine points of dogma forgotten elsewhere in the modern world. And in the müezzin's gallery a young man begins chanting verses from the Koran, his voice wavering on the fine edge between speech and song. While his voice echoes through the mosque all sense of time is lost and one passes the afternoon in a lazy reverie, drifting somewhere between heaven and earth. Soon the mosque fills with sombre shadows, pierced here and there by shafts of moted sunlight, until finally the last rays of the setting sun redden the circlet of windows around the dome. As the shadows turn deep purple with twilight, a mosque servant begins turning on the chandeliers, which now glitter like great wheels of light suspended from the dark empyrean of the dome. Then the old *imam* enters, dressed in his archaic robes and turban, and the faithful assemble for the evening prayer. And thus the hours of the day go by in Beyazıt Camii, just as they have for nearly five centuries past.

The founder, Sultan Beyazıt II, lies buried in a splendid mausoleum which stands in a little garden just behind his mosque. The son and successor of Mehmet the Conqueror, Beyazıt died in 1512 at the age of sixty-six, after having reigned for thirty-one years. He was quite different in character and disposition from his father, being a contemplative man with little taste for war, and during his long reign the Ottoman Empire enjoyed a welcome period of prosperous peace. In his time Beyazıt was known as Sufi, or the Mystic, and after his death his tomb became a place of pilgrimage. Evliya Efendi corroborates this and relates a strange legend concerning the tomb of Sultan Beyazıt.

The mausoleum is now generally visited by the sick, who here find relief from their diseases, because Sultan Beyazıt was a saintly monarch. The last seven years of his life he ate nothing which had life or blood in it. One day, longing much to eat calves' or sheep's feet, he struggled long in this glorious contest with his soul; and when a well-seasoned dish of the feet were placed before him he said unto his soul: 'See, my soul, the feet are before thee; if thou wishest to enjoy them, leave the body and feed on them!' At the same time a living creature was seen to come out of his mouth, which drank of the juice in the dish, and after having satisfied its appetite endeavoured to return from whence it came. But Beyazıt having prevented it with his hand from entering his mouth, it fell to the ground, and the Sultan ordered it to be beaten to death. His pages then entered the room and kicked it to death on the ground. The Mufti of that time decided that as the soul was an essential part of a man, this dead soul should be buried; prayers were performed over it, and the dead soul was interred in a small tomb near Beyazıt's mausoleum. This is the truth of the famous story of Beyazıt II having died twice, and having twice been buried. After this murder of his own soul, the Sultan remained melancholy in the corner of retirement, taking no part nor interest in the affairs of government.

Part of the outer courtyard of Beyazıt Camii is occupied by the renowned Sahaflar Çarşısı, the Market of the Booksellers. The Sahaflar Çarşısı is one of the most picturesque byways in Stamboul; a vine-shaded, sun-dappled courtyard lined with little bookshops, with stalls and barrows outside piled high with cut-rate literary survivors: purple-prosed Victorian novels with vapid heroes and vaporous heroines; obsolete science texts written before the discovery of the atom; spine-less detective stories with the climactic pages missing; repair manuals for machines which no longer exist outside of museums; weird cabbalistic

Fishermen surrounded by child spectators

tracts understandable only to mad Pythagoreans with a knowledge of
Arabic; stacks of *National Geographic*s whose pages have amalgamated
into an amorphous ooze, distorting the faces of happy natives into
snarls – a veritable necropolis of books which never loses its appeal for
the crowds of hopeless bibliomaniacs who silently prowl and pore,
watched over impassively by the white-whiskered booksellers who perch
on tall stools inside their musty shops, surrounded by their beloved but
unmarketable collections of ancient Islamic literature and morocco-
bound sets of the great English classics.

The booksellers in the Sahaflar Çarşısı have been doing business
there since the beginning of the seventeenth century, when they moved
out from their old quarters inside the Covered Bazaar. They were thus
in their present location when Evliya wrote this brief description of the
guild as it passed in the imperial procession of Sultan Murat IV: 'The
Booksellers are 200 in number, with 60 shops. Their patron is Abazer
Ghaffari, who was girded by Selman Pak and is buried in Bokai; he was
170 years old when he died. He was surnamed Abazer (Father of Gold)
by the Prophet because of his riches. The Booksellers adorn their shops
with many thousands of precious books, such as *Multeka*, *Shurer*,
Kusaf, etc.'

The situation has changed somewhat since Evliya's day, for the
precious works now exhibited outside the bookshops in the Sahaflar
Çarşısı bear such illustrious titles as *Business Letters Made Easy*, *The Gear-
Engineer's Annual*, and *Eve and the Monster*. But, never mind, there are still
treasures to be discovered in the Sahaflar Çarşısı; one day I found there
a work for which I had searched for many years – a guide to the New
York City subway system.

The two gateways of the Sahaflar Çarşısı are called the Gate of the
Engravers and the Gate of the Spoon-Makers, named after two of
the guilds who long ago had their headquarters here. The Gate of the
Spoon-Makers gives on to that corner of the outer courtyard opposite
the northern gate of the mosque, a felicitous cloister shaded by the last
of the giant *çınars* still standing in the square. An outdoor teahouse
occupies much of this part of the courtyard, with its kitchen and samovar

housed in a wooden shack built right round the great tree itself. Tradition has it that this teahouse was once a hang-out for the Janissaries, whose main barracks stood near Beyazıt Square until their destruction in 1826. Nowadays, students from Istanbul University rest their overburdened minds here between classes, and over their tea-glasses discuss the affairs of the world with the terrific intensity given only to young theorists. One of them leans over and asks me if I have read Dostoevski. I groan silently and say yes, and while the weighty discussion proceeds on its boring and inexorable course, I notice that a herd of sheep has begun to wander among the tables of the teahouse. I look around and soon locate their owner, a peasant clothed in a patchwork suit stitched together from the inherited rags of his village ancestors. He is standing at the edge of a crowd in the Flea Market, scratching himself absently as he gawks at a huckster selling inflatable rubber giraffes. I can see the huckster's hands expand as he tells the crowd of the enormous size to which giraffes grow in their native habitat, and of the great height to which this rubber giraffe would grow too, if only one blew into it hard and long enough. And above the bleating of sheep and the voices of students arguing about socialism, I hear the climax of the huckster's pitch as he announces the absurdly low price of the inflatable giraffe in a shrill giraffe-like voice. These are the things one is liable to see and hear in Beyazıt Square, seated under that giant *çınar* which a poet once called the Tree of Idleness.

The faithful at prayer

9

The Moon of Ramazan

Istanbul regulates its seasons according to the orbits of both the sun and the moon. Along with all other modern cities, Istanbul defines its civic year in accordance with the Gregorian solar calendar, while its religious year, as Evliya would say, is regulated by the stations of the moon. And since, as astronomers inform us, the solar and lunar years differ in length by about ten days, the religious and civic seasons rotate with respect to one another, with a periodicity of thirty-six years. Straddling two continents and poised hesitatingly between two worlds, Istanbul nevertheless enjoys the holidays of two incommensurable calendars.

The Islamic month begins with the first appearance of the sickle moon on the western horizon shortly after sunset. In olden times the precise occasion of the lunar reappearance was often a matter of dispute between mosque astronomers, depending upon the weather and their often uncertain eyesight. But today the dates for the beginnings of the lunar months have been computed beforehand with great exactitude, and mosque astronomers need no longer concern themselves with matters of chronology. (The few who remain sometimes serve as clock-repairmen for the people of the neighbourhood.)

The most important period of the Islamic year is Ramazan, the ninth and sacred month. This month was designated as sacred by the Prophet Mohammed because of the epiphanies and revelations accorded him during the period of Ramazan; the first chapter of the Koran was revealed to him on the twentieth and the remainder on the twenty-seventh, at which time Mohammed ascended into heaven for a while. Accordingly, the Prophet set aside the month of Ramazan as a time of prayer and fasting, in commemoration of those great events which gave rise to the Islamic religion. The faithful were directed to partake of neither food nor drink from sunrise to sunset for the twenty-nine days of Ramazan each year, and to perform special prayers and good works during that time. Although many modern Stamboullus no longer observe these practices, the poor and the peasants, with whom this town abounds, hold to them religiously.

An old traveller to Stamboul once remarked that Ramazan there was a Lent lined with Carnival. There is still some truth to this, although Ramazan in Stamboul has little of the guilt-laden gloom of Lent nor the bacchanalian mirth of Carnival. It is just that while the days of Ramazan are apt to be dull and cheerless, the evenings are quite festive and even gay. During the long, foodless, drinkless and cigaretteless days of Ramazan, tempers are liable to be a trifle short and civic patience thin, with teahouses, cafés, shops and restaurants empty, and the life of the town lacking something of its normal boisterous spirit. The mosques are full, however, and one is then astonished to find how strong a religious spirit still exists in this cynical town, especially in its poorer quarters. Then, in late afternoon, the town begins to come back to life again, and there is a sense of expectancy in the air. Food shops and greengrocers become crowded with excited and impatient women, bakeries fire up their ovens while long lines of salivating customers form outside, butcher shops resound with the whack of cleavers and the pounding of mallets, coveys of waiters assemble at the doors of restaurants and cafés, the streets are jammed with rattletrap buses and public taxis bouncing home across the cobbles, and from the stovepipe thickets of the *ahşap evleri* an aromatic cloud rises above the town. And then, quite suddenly, a hush falls over the entire city. We stop what we are doing and look off towards the western horizon, where the swollen orange sun is now completing its daily course, sinking into the Sea of Marmara. When the last segment of the solar disc has disappeared we hear the echoing report of a cannon firing from the Selimiye army barracks across the straits in Kadıköy. The day and its fast are ended and the town suddenly returns to life. Restaurants fill with hungry workers cramming huge gobs of food into their mouths, served by harassed waiters who eat on the run and cooks who sup while they stir soup, carve meat and turn sputtering spits. Crowds of tired men rush towards their homes carrying great steaming layers of *pide*, the flat unleavened bread of Ramazan, while their families wait poised around tables loaded down with mounds of food. Arriving home, the man of the house takes his place at the head of the table, kisses the *pide* and presses it reverentially to his forehead, and then he and his family begin to devour the food before them. It is the time of *iftar*, the evening meal, which in this holy month takes on the appearance of a folk-sacrament.

After the evening meal is finished, the family sits together in the kitchen or the living-room, if they have one, and passes the evening there together, eating sweets and sherbets till well past midnight. The more pious visit their neighbourhood mosque for the special night-prayer of Ramazan, the *teravih namazı*, and listen to recitals of the Koran, which is read through in its entirety during the month. The interiors of the mosques are specially decorated, the *mimber* is hung with green embroidered silks, and all of the lamps and chandeliers are lit, while outside the domes, arches and minarets are outlined in lights. The larger mosques advertise pious sentiments in lights strung between their minarets. *'Merhaba!'* (Hello!), they say on the first night, to be succeeded on following nights by such luminous slogans as: 'Oh Ramazan!' 'Begin with the name of God,' or 'God is the Lord of the Universe!' etc., and finally, on the last night of Ramazan, *'Allahaısmarladık!'* (May God keep you!). Thereby the old town of Stamboul, which in other seasons is darkened and asleep three hours after sunset, is in the holy month a city of lights; sparkling domes and spires glittering over the constellations of glowing tenement-windows, even the cobbles luminous under the moon of Ramazan.

Ramazan nights are not nearly so gay in modern Istanbul as they were in past generations. In the old days the coffee-houses in town were lavishly decorated during the month of Ramazan and featured special nocturnal entertainments. These included special performances of *Karagöz*, the shadow-puppets, *Orta Oyunu*, the old Turkish folk-theatre, recitals of music and poetry by the Aşıklar the traditional Turkish bards, folk-tales by the Meddahlar, or storytellers, performances by Gypsy dancers and singers, or exhibitions by mimics, magicians, conjurors, fire-eaters, sword-swallowers, and other tricksters, freaks, prodigies and marvels. Here, for example, is Evliya Efendi's description of two of the great entertainers of his day:

In Sultan Murat's time, the chief of all the mimics was Hasan-zadeh, the player of Chinese shades, who performed twice a week in the Sultan's presence. He was a skilful gentleman, who knew Arabic, Persian and music, in which he was a second Faryabi. He played the Chinese shades, he wrote beautiful Ta'lik, and was a good fireworker. In short, like Jemshid, he was versed in a thousand arts and sciences. Being extremely given to women, he invented all the famous scenes of Karagöz, which are known by the names of The Fine Girl's Play, The Dumb Man's Play, The Arab Beggar's Play, and The Gentleman Heritage-Eater's Play. In the first of these, Jowan Nigar, the fine girl, is violated in the bath by some strolling gentlemen and Karagöz is carried naked into the street. In short, he has contrived no less than three hundred plays for the Chinese shades, in which he was out-rivalled by nobody, and though all his farces and plays were intended in a mystical sense, yet the spectators always died with laughter. When he came forth from the puppet-theatre to breathe a little, he drank four cups of coffee to restore himself, and began then in good humour to play scenes on the stage himself, by which he set all the spectators in an uproar of laughter. During forty-seven years I have seen all kinds of mimics, but no one so funny, clever and witty as he. Another mimic of this kind, who was also a janissary of the regiment of Zagharji, was a prince of speech who amused Sultan Murat by reading the satires of Sheikh Zadeh in twelve different languages, representing the scenes of an opium-eater, a dervish and a grocer. The dervish having cursed the grocer's honey for having been refused a bit of it, all those who bought and ate of it became subject to colic and wind, so that they went at last to the judge, who upon tasting the honey, became afflicted in a similar manner. In this way the tribunal fills with eleven persons, all attacked with the same disease, which affords one of the most comical scenes of Turkish comedy.

Sad to say, these fabulous coffee-house entertainments are now a thing of the past and have all but disappeared from the life of Stamboul. Although *Karagöz* is still performed in conventional theatres during Ramazan, it is not quite the same as the old-fashioned, uncensored and uninhibited coffee-house show. These days one can no longer hope to see priapic-armed old Karagöz carried naked from the bath after the fine girl has been violated by the gentleman strollers.

Nor does one often find the Meddahlar, or traditional storytellers, sitting where they used to on the stage of an old-fashioned coffee-house. In times past the Meddah held the coffee-house audience in rapt attention through the evening as he recited one of the typical old Turkish folk-tales, the stories which began with such ritual introductions as this: 'Once upon a time God's servants were many, very long ago the sifter was in the hay, the camel was a pedlar, the mouse a hairdresser, the donkey was the bearer of the king's stamp and the mule an armourer. When I shook my mother's cradle the drunkard Mustafa became angry, grew white whiskers, black whiskers, yellow whiskers. If I am a butcher I cannot use my knife, if I am a blacksmith I cannot shoe a mule, if I enter a hamam I cannot find the soap. I came from the river, I came from the hill, I entered a tree and what did I see but a woman sitting inside. The woman stood up, looked at my face and we went off together, turning neither to left nor right. We went far, we went near. We travelled on for six months and an autumn, passing rivers and hills, and we looked back and saw that we had travelled the distance of a barley plant. So then let me tell you a story. The story began . . . ' And perhaps half the audience had fallen asleep before the ritual conclusion, hours later, when the Meddah finally said: 'Three apples fell from the sky to those who have a will, and so my story ends.'

So they passed the long nights of Ramazan in old Stamboul. And then an hour or so before dawn the *bekçi*, or neighbourhood watchmen, marched through the streets pounding their drums to wake the faithful for *sahur*, the pre-dawn meal, when everyone fills himself in preparation for the long, empty day. This old custom still survives in many of the poorer districts of Stamboul. The drum awakens the infidel too, and he stumbles out on to his balcony to see lights coming on all over the city, hears the tired voices of women rousing their families, and, later, their animated chatter as they gather round the breakfast table. Then the empty streets echo with the resonant cries of müezzins announcing to the faithful that it is time for *imsak namazı*, the morning prayer. Soon afterwards, when the light has grown strong enough so that an old *imam* can distinguish a white hair from a black one, the report of the Ramazan cannon resounds once again throughout the city. Another day of Ramazan has begun and the fast called 'empty-belly' is resumed.

The most sacred time in Ramazan comes on the eve of the twenty-seventh of the month. This is known as *Kadir Gecesi*, the Night of Power, and commemorates the Miraç, or the ascension of the Prophet Mohammed into heaven. The Night of Power is thought to be the most dread and mysterious of all the nights in the year. All the elements in nature – men, animals, plants and even inanimate objects, are said to feel the mystical forces generated on that night, and to give token, in some unknown way, of their subservience to the omnipotent creator. It is believed, too, that on this night there are written down in the Book of Fate the names of those who are to die during the coming year. As the Koran itself says of the Night of Power: 'In the name of the most merciful God: "Verily we sent down the Koran in the night of al'Kadir. And what shall make thee understand how excellent is the night of al'Kadir? The night of al'Kadir is better than a thousand months. Therein do the angels descend and the spirit of Gabriel, also, by the permission of their Lord, with his decrees concerning every matter. It is peace till the rising of the morn." '

And from Evliya Efendi we have a wondrous description of the Miraç itself:

The Prophet being fifty-one years old and residing at Mecca in the house of Omni Hani, received from Gabriel the invitation to the

Stone carving at the entrance to a graveyard

Miraç, the Heavenly Visit, and was given the celestial horse called Refref. They shook hands together as brethren and Gabriel said: 'Oh Prophet, the Lord's greetings to thee;' he says: 'Thou shall mount the celestial conveyance, gird thy limbs with this silken handkerchief of paradise, and look upon the throne, the firmament, the table of fate and the pen, on the eight paradises, the eighteen thousand worlds, and my own perfection.' The Prophet, on the night of the ascension, having seen the eighteen thousand worlds, approached the person of God himself . . . Thus invested he appeared before the throne and spoke with the Lord, as some say 21,000 words, as others say 70,000 words. Returning from this ascension on the same night to his house of Omni Hani, he found his bed still warm . . . This great miracle having become the talk of the Prophet's friends, he could not continue to live on good terms with the unbelievers of Mecca, and he fled with his companions to Medina, where he remained for ten years.

To sense something of the mystical power of *Kadir Gecesi*, one must visit one of the imperial mosques in Stamboul on that night. After the evening prayer is concluded the mosque fills to overflowing; kerchiefed women squatting in the galleries to side and rear, the nave packed with a mass of kneeling men, choirs of singers and chanters sitting cross-legged in their marble loggias, the robed and turbaned *imam* standing on the top step of the *mimber*, all illuminated by galaxies of glowing lamps suspended from the great dome. Then begins the long liturgy of *Kadir Gecesi*, the most moving of all Moslem ceremonies. While the *imam* pronounces the prayers, the massed ranks of the faithful perform together the ritual genuflections, and the chanters of the Koran recite in a high and dissonant minor key, punctuated at intervals by fervent roars of 'Allah!' and 'Amin!' from the congregation. Then, quite suddenly, the singers burst forth into a melody of quite astonishing lyric beauty, and the packed crowd sways back and forth, humming and singing in concert with the choirs. At this moment even the infidel senses something of the great power and mystery of *Kadir Gecesi*.

The twenty-ninth and last night of Ramazan is called *Arife Gecesi*. On this night the mantle of the Prophet is taken from its place of safe-keeping and exhibited to the faithful in the mosque of Hirkai Şeref. This night is also the traditional occasion for the bestowal of *zekât*, in which the rich are directed to bestow one-fortieth of their wealth upon the poor. Since the inception of the graduated income tax, however, wealthy Stamboullus have abandoned this ancient philanthropic custom. And although the faithful flock into the mosques on this night, they are perhaps more concerned with their last-minute shopping for the holidays, and flock in even greater numbers to the local shops and markets. For on the morrow begins the feast of *Şeker Bayramı*, celebrating the end of Ramazan and its long days of empty-bellied fasting.

Şeker Bayramı, the Sweet or Sugar Holiday, is the most festive and joyous of all seasons in Stamboul, and is for Moslems a combination of Thanksgiving Day, Christmas and New Year's Day, all rolled into one. It is a time for feasting and for parties, for visiting between relatives and friends, and for exchanging presents. It is also a time for presenting tips and gifts to servants and tradesmen for services rendered during the preceding year. Prominent among the hordes of recipients who present themselves at this time are the *bekçi*, who are particularly to be thanked for their help in rousing the faithful for the morning meal during Ramazan. The infidel is advised to tip the *bekçi* too, if only in gratitude that his slumbers will not be interrupted before dawn until the following Ramazan.

Aşık İhsani, a wandering minstrel

10

Wandering Minstrels

Aşık İhsani is one of the last of the Meydan Şairleri, the saz-playing poet-minstrels who recite and sing their works in the squares and mosque-courtyards of Stamboul. He is adorned with the name of Aşık, or Lover, because his poetry and his songs are concerned mostly with the subject of love. He follows a tradition which is centuries old; the Aşıklar, or wandering love-poets, have been singing in the towns of Anatolia for more than five hundred years. Many of the Aşıklar come from the eastern regions of Turkey, although their wanderings have taken them in time to all parts of the country. In fact, the Aşıklar can hardly be said to have a home at all, for they live where their music takes them and sleep beside their saz in the room where they last played. In their long wanderings they have become the folk-heroes of Turkey, the free men who walk into town and sing and say what they please, criticising the sultan, the ağa, the governor, the landlord or the police, if those authorities have been cruel or unjust. And so their repertoire has come to include many topics besides that of love, for the Turkish peasants to whom they sing had little of love from those who ruled them, but much injustice and cruel neglect. But the songs of the Aşıklar always return in the end to the subject of love; mystical, sad, hopeless and unrequited love, for such is the nature of Anatolian life, and it is such songs that the Turkish peasant longs to hear. As Evliya Efendi wrote, speaking of the wandering minstrels of his own time: 'These players are possessed of the particular skill to evoke by their songs the remembrance of absent friends and distant countries, so that the souls of their hearers grow melancholy.'

These wandering minstrels receive their training in much the same way as an ordinary Turkish workman. The young poet is apprenticed to a journeyman Aşık, from whom he learns to play the saz and to acquire the metre and rhyme and lore of his art. He also spends these years in building up his store of poems and songs; and more important still, in developing that most essential skill of the Aşıklar, their ability to compose extemporaneous poems and songs on any subject. Then, when his apprenticeship is completed, the young minstrel receives from his master his saz and his poet-lover's name and heads off down the roads of Turkey.

In earlier times most large towns in Turkey had their own resident Aşık, and set aside a room for his use. When another wandering Aşık arrived in town a contest, or *atışma*, was arranged between the two, usually in the *kahvehane*. In the *atışma*, each Aşık takes his saz and seats himself upon a stool, the two facing one another in the centre of the room, surrounded by the crowd. Then, bowing to one another, they sing and recite in turn. The opening songs are usually of mystical love, and the subject of the first player's song suggests that of the other so that a duel evolves, with each responding to the other's song, trying to outdo him in imagery and wit and musical skill, evoking from the admiring crowd cries of '*Aman!*' (Alas!), '*Kuzum!*' (My lamb!), '*Canim!*' (My soul!), or even '*Ah minel aşk!*' (Alas what a tyrant is love!). After a time, the duel becomes more pointed and the poets begin to insult one another in song, and it is the one who destroys his opponent with these rhyming insults who is often adjudged the winner. Aşık İhsani and Aşık Şemsi took each other on in such an *atışma* in Stamboul several years ago. İhsani seemed clearly ahead during the poetry recitations and in the love songs, for he is easily the most romantic-looking of all Aşıklar: a great leonine head on the body of a beautiful child, a magnificent mane of wavy raven hair merging with his beard and falling down over his chest and shoulders, a powerful forehead corrugated with wrinkles, a splendid, prow-shaped Semitic nose, and hypnotic black eyes that fix the spectator and seduce him to the belief that İhsani is singing to him alone – obviously not the sort of man with whom one should lightly cross a saz. But it is easy to parody the figure and extravagant expressions of such an erotic-looking character, and so Şemsi began to score heavily off İhsani when the duel reached the stage of mockery and insult. In fact, it was İhsani's beautiful mane of raven hair that got him into the most serious difficulty; for, as beautiful as it is, it has the same colour and texture as that of the ubiquitous black goat of Turkey. And so in Şemsi's song İhsani became a saz-playing black goat. The crowd roared with laughter at the musical image of goat-İhsani leaping from rock to rock in the hills and eating the tender leaves of mountain trees and eventually falling to Şemsi's hand to be sacrificed and to have his skin flayed and his joints grilled and eaten by Şemsi, who afterwards, when full, would take his ease upon a rug woven from İhsani's rich, black goat-hair, where he would recline and play his saz and sing songs of love to İhsani's woman. Then, in the final verses of his song, carried away by his soaring wit and intoxicated by his apparent success, Şemsi threw back his head and gazed up at an imaginary moon on the coffee-house ceiling, and sang in what he believed to be tremulous and love-stricken tones of profound passion. But he had, of course, outdone himself, and as soon as İhsani began his final response Şemsi knew that he had gone a bit too far. For İhsani likened Şemsi to a starved and mangy dog baying at the moon, and so, far from even hoping to sit singing songs of love to İhsani's woman, he would more likely receive from her scraps of garbage at the kitchen door, and the only ones who would reply to his moon-howling would be a chorus of contemptuous cats on the *kahvehane* roof. When İhsani had finished his song, Şemsi knew that he was well-beaten in both love and insult. And so he most graciously rose from his stool, walked across to kiss İhsani's hand, and pressed it to his forehead in an affectionate token of victory. İhsani, though, retained his sad romantic look through all of this, for he is a poet-lover, and poetic love is a very melancholy enterprise when practised in the antique manner of the Aşıklar.

Aşık İhsani is most often to be seen in the courtyard of the mosque of Nuruosmaniye. He earns his way in life by selling little paperback volumes of his poems and songs; they are very popular among the village people who come to Istanbul. He sits under a plane-tree in the courtyard, surrounded by these peasants, reciting his old poems and creating new ones, and singing love songs while he plays upon his saz. He always begins by telling of how he began his long quest which has taken him through all the towns of Turkey. He tells of a dream he had one night, many years ago, when he was sleeping on the slopes of Nimrut Dağı. He dreamt that he was walking along a road in early evening and that he came upon a young girl seated by the side of a well. Although the girl wore a violet *yaşmak*, or veil, about her face, he could tell from her eyes and her hair that she was most beautiful. İhsani sat down beside her and began to play upon his saz and sing of love. When he had finished his song the girl drew aside her *yaşmak* and smiled at him. She told him that her name was Güllüşah and that she would wait for him until he found her again, although many years might pass. Alas! when İhsani awoke the beautiful Güllüşah was no longer there and so he took up his bundle and his saz and began to look for her.

At this point in the narrative İhsani begins to sing the song called *Mor Yaşmaklım* (My One with the Violet *Yaşmak*) while his young assistant passes through the crowd selling little volumes of İhsani's poems; the cover shows İhsani sleeping with his saz by his side, while a dream – Güllüşah – floats on a cloud overhead.

'My one with the violet *yaşmak*, if you come to me, come without speaking,' he sings, and the peasant women dab at their eyes with their own *yaşmak*. 'Come, O my life, my day, my light; my paradise, my home, my *houri*./ I am waiting for the evening; dim your light and come.' '*Aman, Aman!*' cries an old woman in the crowd. İhsani then looks deeply into the eyes of every unloved peasant woman in the crowd and sings the last line of his song: 'Come, let not your feet be hurt, my woman, my eyes make a path for you./Come, stepping over them.' And the peasant women weep behind their veils as they buy every last sentimental volume of İhsani's poems.

Aşik İhsani searched for his love for seven long years, sadly playing his saz and singing of his lost Güllüşah through all the towns of eastern Turkey. He found her at last one day in Diyarbakır, sitting by the side of a well in early evening, wearing a violet *yaşmak*. She is with him today in the courtyard of the Nuruosmaniye Mosque as he sadly plays his saz and sings of his long wanderings. The beautiful Güllüşah sits by İhsani's side, wearing her violet *yaşmak*, looking bored with it all.

But, sad to say, Aşık İhsani no longer sings of love these days. Some time ago he was arrested by the police and charged with being a Communist. In court he composed and sang a song in protest, proclaiming that he was not a thief or a murderer but only a common man making his way in the world with his simple skills, like any worker. But the police beat him for his song and threw him into prison, shaving off his hair and beard and smashing his saz, thinking thus to break his spirit and silence him. İhsani has since been freed, but his songs now are bitter and angry, and the words 'police' and 'politicians' often occur, accompanied by symbolic spitting upon the ground. Most of the other remaining Aşıklar of Turkey have also come under suspicion and have been harassed by the police; Aşık İzzet, Aşık Ruhi Su, Aşık Şemsi, Aşık Fermani and many others. Their poems, too, have become songs of protest and they seldom sing of love these days. Only the oldest of all the Aşıklar, Aşık Veysel, seemed to have remained undisturbed by these changes. Aşık Veysel, who has since died in his native village near Kayseri, knew little of cities and politics. He was blind since childhood and spent his whole life among the village people of Anatolia, sharing their labours, their poverty, their sadness and their occasional joy. In his songs and poems Aşık Veysel celebrated the simple and immemorial events of village life: birth, death, love, marriage, the beauty of wild flowers in summer, the friendship between old men. And when he sang of the first nightingale in April, his cracked and wavering old voice produced that ache of love and sadness which the nightingale itself evokes, particularly in an Anatolian spring.

Aşık İhsani still sings and plays his saz in the courtyard of the Nuruosmaniye Mosque. Each time I see him there I feel that when he and his fellow minstrels have finished their songs, as they surely will within this generation, Turkey will have lost for ever one of the most distinctive and lovely traditions from its past. The beautiful Güllüşah still sits there by İhsani's side, but he no longer tells of his long search for her; instead he sings of the eternal sorrows of the Turkish people. It is for this reason that İhsani's songs now are sadder than they ever were before, when he sang only of love.

The Goose Fountain

11

The Street of the Dwarf's Fountain

The Street of the Dwarf's Fountain is one of the most picturesque in Stamboul, wandering, as it does, through the venerable district of Şehzadebaşı. If we stroll along this ancient street we come across a fascinating variety of structures from different periods in the city's past. The Street of the Dwarf's Fountain begins in the square outside the Byzantine church of the Kyriotissa, whose origins go back as far as the sixth century. It then passes an old Turkish graveyard which centres around the tomb of a Turkish warrior-saint who was killed during the siege of Constantinople in 1453. The street then runs beside the Roman aqueduct of Valens, built in the second half of the fourth century. Under the lower arches of the aqueduct we see some of the most imaginative of those wooden shanties built by the folk-architects of Stamboul. One, a modern stylite, has even perched his shack high above the street in the former watercourse of the aqueduct itself. Another has built a veritable sliver of a shanty atop a tapering ruin – a house so narrow that the owner must needs sleep on his side, and if he has a fat wife she must seek shelter elsewhere. Walking along this wondrous street we pass in turn a ruined mosque, an abandoned medrese, or school of Islamic theology, a cat and dog hospital, and a coffin-maker's shop, all standing side-by-side under the arches of the Roman aqueduct. Then finally we come to the wall-fountain after which the street is named. This fountain was constructed in 1590 by one Mehmet Ağa, a minor functionary in the court of Sultan Murat III. The inscription on the fountain reads: 'The dwarf Mehmet Ağa, that lucky fellow of good fortune, has commissioned this fountain and made it flow for God's sake.' Nearby is the fountain of his colleague, Süleyman Ağa the Mute. The inscription here reads: 'Süleyman Ağa, an esteemed person, the favourite mute of Sultan Murat, built this fountain for the good of others, and Sai the poet commemorated the date when its waters began to flow (AH994, or AD1586).'

The fountains of the Dwarf and the Mute are examples of the minor pious foundations which were established by well-off Osmanlis, for the good of their souls and the benefit of their fellow Stamboullus. The picturesque appearance of Şehzadebaşı. owes much to the various pious foundations with which the neighbourhood is richly endowed, many of them still serving the people of Stamboul as they have for centuries past. Perhaps the most beautiful of these is to be found on the Avenue of Dede Efendi, which intersects the Street of the Dwarf's Fountain about midway along its course. This is the foundation of Damat İbrahim Paşa, built in the first half of the eighteenth century. This little complex consists only of a *dar-ül-hadis*, or school of tradition, now used as an eye-clinic, a small mosque, and the tomb of the founder, who is buried in the garden beside his school. Outside his graveyard the founder has left one additional benefaction for the people of Stamboul. This is a *sebil*, or enclosed water-fountain, which is set into the graveyard wall at the corner of the street. These *sebils* were once used to distribute water free to thirsty passers-by. *Sebil* means literally 'way' or 'path', and to construct a *sebil* was to build a path for oneself to paradise. These *sebils* were usually extremely attractive, with ornate gilded bronze grilles and carved and sculptured marble façades. The *sebil* of Damat İbrahim Paşa is semi-circular in form, with four windows framed in engaged marble columns and screened with gilded bronze grilles, all curving gracefully around the corner; it was a favourite with romantic etchers of the last century. The *sebil* was in service up until a generation ago, but now it is being used as a fruit seller's stall. The colourful piles of apples and oranges artistically stacked on the marble steps of the *sebil* provide a striking contrast with the marble fruit and flowers in the baroque relief-work behind them. The effect would surely have delighted Damat İbrahim Paşa, the founder. İbrahim Paşa was the son-in-law (*damat*) of Sultan Ahmet III and served as his Grand Vezir from 1718 until 1730, those golden years of the Tulip Age, when the Sultan and his court patterned themselves on a garden of flowers. That delightful epoch ended on September 20th, 1730, when Sultan Ahmet was deposed by the Janissaries and İbrahim Paşa was strangled by the Chief Executioner. The beautiful *sebil* standing outside his tomb is a fitting monument to the chief minister of the Tulip King. Although his *sebil* no longer distributes free water, it still gratifies passers-by with its beauty. For that reason alone it should provide a path to paradise for its departed donor.

Fountains and *sebils* such as these are to be found by the hundreds in all parts of the city. In his *Seyahatname* Evliya lists scores of the most important street-fountains and *sebil* of his day, and nearly all of them are still in existence. None of the *sebil* are now functioning, but almost all of the fountains, or *çeşme* are still in use. For centuries these *çeşme* were the only source of water for the common people of Stamboul, and even now there are many sections of the city which still depend mainly upon them. They have probably been of more real service to Stamboullus than all of the other pious foundations taken together.

The fountains of Istanbul are totally different from those of Rome. Here there are no dramatic sculptured figures, no allegorical river gods and spouting cherubs, no elaborate cascades and pools. The fountains of Istanbul are simple and utilitarian, but nonetheless they are often quite beautiful. In their most basic form they consist of merely a niche set into a wall, with water flowing from a spout into a marble basin. The water-spout is set into a marble tablet called the mirror-stone, which is often decorated with floral or geometrical designs in low relief. The niche is usually framed in an arch and the façade of the surrounding wall is sheathed in marble which is decorated in the same design as is the mirror-stone. At the top of this façade there is always a calligraphic inscription giving the name of the donor and the date of construction. These inscriptions are often in the form of chronograms, where the numerical value of the Arabic letters gives the pertinent information. A typical example of such a chronogram can be seen on the fountain of Ahi Durmuş Baba near Beyazıt Square. The first part of the inscription informs us that the donor of the fountain was Ahi Durmuş Baba, who

served as a water-carrier in the army of Sultan Beyazıt II. The chronogram appears in the last phrase of the inscription, which reads: 'Heaven
will be his place'. A clever Arabic scholar equipped with a slide rule can
then compute the date of the construction as AH916, or AD1511. Many
of these inscriptions are much more elaborate, containing references to
the Four Fountains of Paradise and the pool Kevser into which they
flow; the sacred well of Zemzem in Mecca, which the angel Gabriel
opened for the wife of Abraham; the Fountain of Life, discovered by
the fabulous Hızırilyas; or the battle of Kerbala, where Hüseyin and his
companions died of thirst. An example of such an elaborate chronogram
is the one which appears on the baroque fountain which stands in the
Square of the White Moustache: 'When the mother of Ali Paşa, Vezir in
the reign of Sultan Mahmut I, quenched the thirst of the people with the
pure and clear water of her charity, Riza of Beşiktaş, a Nakşibendi
dervish, uttered the following epigram: "Come and drink the water of
eternal life from this fountain"' (AH1157, or AD1741). These chronograms became a favourite art form for Ottomam poets and they vied
with one another in composing clever and original epigrams. The ideal
chronogram, as far as they were concerned, would not only give the
name of the donor and the date of the construction, but would also
advertise the poetic talents of the composer. An example of this sort of
epigram is found on the monumental street-fountain of Sultan Ahmet
III. The inscription is by the celebrated poet Sayit Wehbi; in ornate
golden letters he praises the fountain and compares its waters with those
of the holy spring Zemzem and of the sacred *selsebil* of paradise. The
inscription then ends with these modest lines: 'Seyit Wehbi Efendi, the
most distinguished among the word-wizards of the age, strung these
pearls on the thread of his verse and joined together the two lines of the
chronographic distich, like two sweet almonds, breast to breast: "With
what a wall has Sultan Ahmet dammed the waters! For of astonishment
stops the flood in the midst of its course"' (AH1139, or AD1728).
Other chronographers managed to do their job in true epigrammatic
style without boasting or elaboration; as, for example, on the fountain
of Semiz Ali Paşa. The chronogram on this fountain refers to the historic

Fountain at Tophane

river Şatt al Arap, the confluence of the Tigris and the Euphrates. It reads: 'The water of this fountain flows like the waters of Şatt. When Baghdad hears the sound its mouth waters!' (AH965, or AD1558). One of my favourite inscriptions is the one which appears on a simple little fountain which stands in the market area near the Galata Bridge. It makes no pretence to wit or poetry, but gives only this common-sense admonition to those who make use of its waters: 'Never quarrel nor argue with your neighbour over this water; let him take some and you some too!'

What is perhaps the oldest of all the street-fountains in Istanbul is to be found just outside the Belgrade Gate. This is the Kazlı Çeşme, or Goose Fountain, so named because it is decorated with the figure in low relief of a rather gay-looking, long-necked goose. The Goose Fountain, which gives its name to the surrounding neighbourhood, is believed to date back to the days of Byzantium. An inscription tells us that the fountain was restored in the year 1546 by a certain Mehmet Bey. This poetic inscription concludes with a cheery greeting from the benefactor: 'Good health to friends who drink here!'

One of the loveliest street-fountains in Stamboul stands in the district of the White Moustache, a picturesque quarter rarely if ever visited by tourists, although it is just behind the Blue Mosque. The fountain stands in the village square and is the principal source of water for this impoverished but happy neighbourhood. Although it might seem just an ordinary *çeşme*, of the type seen all over town, this fountain is distinguished by its exceedingly beautiful decorations in low relief, all in the finest baroque style. The mirror-stone is decorated with the silhouettes of wind-bent cypresses; beside and above them are represented bowls of fruit and flowering plants, all framed in a frieze of intertwined vines. The beauty of the fountain is enhanced by the accidental artistry of two centuries of human use; the stone flowers highlighted by the soot of supper fires; the marble seats beside the fountain worn into familiar saddle shapes by generations of gossiping women; the hollow in the mirror-stone into which your hand fits when you stoop to take a drink. This fountain has been the focus of life in the square since the day it was built in the year 1745. For this is one of those fortunate Stamboul neighbourhoods which has not yet been ruined by progress. And although it is inconvenient not to have running water in the house, the fountain in the square compensates for it, serving as a laundry and ladies' forum, children's bath, restaurant-sink, horse-trough and ablution fountain. One must sit for a few hours in one of the cafés on the square to appreciate how vital is this fountain to the life of the quarter; to see the children who stop there to drink during their games in the square; the women who chat there while waiting for their water-jars to fill; the exhausted pedlars who cool themselves under the water-tap and then sit back with their wet heads resting against the baroque vine-leaves and count the pitiful handful of coins which they have earned in their long day's labour. When we sit in the square, sipping our rakı, we think about all the timeless activities nourished by this old fountain. We consider, too, the countless other ways in which this old town has managed to retain some of the rich and humane qualities which have been lost in modern cities. We were talking of these things one afternoon, in the Square of the White Moustache, when we noticed a young girl standing beside the fountain. She had paused for a moment to speak to a friend and stood there with one hand on her hip and the other curving in a graceful bow to hold the amphora she was bearing on her shoulder, in the archaic posture reminiscent of an Attic frieze – classic beauty at the well, here in rough old Stamboul.

Children playing sek-sek

12

Street Games

In his account of the Imperial Procession of Murat IV, Evliya Efendi describes the schoolboys of Stamboul, 'whose number is known only to God'. He tells us that the Corporation of Schoolboys came immediately after that of the Messengers of Death and the Washers of Corpses and that they were followed by the Corporation of Beggars. 'These boys great and small make themselves caps of paper and play upon tambourines, which they carry in their hands; in this manner they accompany the public procession, dancing and frolicking in a thousand ways. They are like an army of Jinns.' Then, towards the very end of the parade, in the regiment made up of 'The Fools and Mimics of Constantinople', Evliya describes the 'mischievous boys of the town, who have exhausted seventy cups of the poison of life and misrule, and who crowd together and play, day and night'. The schoolboys of Stamboul would not seem to have changed in their antics or habits in the three centuries since Evliya's time.

I was reminded of these lines from Evliya one afternoon while walking through the district called Wednesday. The district takes its name from the riotous travelling market which throngs its streets each week on that day, but since I was strolling on a Friday afternoon the neighbourhood was quiet and serene. It was, that is, until I came to the corner of the Street of the White Turban, where I came upon a comical scene involving Evliya's mischievous boys of the town. It seems, as I was told afterwards by an old lady, that a new bakery had just opened on the street that morning. According to an old Turkish tradition, the baker had celebrated the opening of his shop by distributing free bread to all the housewives in the neighbourhood. Now, in the afternoon, with all

of his potential customers favourably disposed towards him, the baker
dreamed of the long years of profitable trade ahead. But then, at four
o'clock in the afternoon, the large elementary school at the end of the
street opened and released its ravenous hordes of small boys. This
starving rabble army marched straight to the new bakery, drawn there
by the tantalising odours of hot bread and the rumours of free loaves
which had been rising all day to their schoolroom windows. The poor
baker stood alone at the door of his shop, a terrified Horatio armed only
with a long dough-paddle. He held off the boy-army briefly, but then
they overcame him and poured into his bakery, quickly over-running
the dough-white assistants who formed the interior defences. The boys
then gorged themselves on hot rolls and cakes, stuffed layers of flat *pide*
inside their shirts, and loaded their school-bags with long loaves of
frangala. When they had stripped the ovens, trays and bread-rack, their
leader shrilly whistled the signal of retreat and fled the ransacked bakery.
But the baker had now recovered and began to drub the rearguard with
his dough-paddle in an attempt to recover some of the loot. Then the
boy-captain, equipped with paper-bag helmet, garbage-lid shield and
broomstick-sword, engaged the baker in single combat to cover the
retreat of his mini-army, who supported him in turn by bombarding the
baker with a barrage of half-eaten rolls. The baker raised his dough-
paddle and took a mighty swipe, but alas it missed and only dislodged
his adversary's paper helmet. The young captain, who had learned his
swordsman's art watching Errol Flynn in the neighbourhood cinema,
lunged forward and deftly prodded the baker's rotund belly with his
broomstick, thus deflating his opponent and ending the uneven battle.
The mischievous schoolboys of Stamboul had won the day once again.

The streets of the city are thus controlled by the children of Stamboul
during the hours when they are free. When wandering through the town
in those hours, then, it is advisable to be accompanied by a child, who
will act as guide, guard, consul and interpreter. This young *dragoman* will
explain to you the marvellous arcane lore of Stamboul kids, verse you in
that secret language which they call *kuşdili*, or bird-talk, interpret for you
the curious and funny chalk diagrams and drawings which deface all the

walls and side walks of the town. He will reveal hiding-places unknown to grown-ups, introduce you into his clubs, social and athletic, allow you to watch his street-games and perhaps even invite you to play, if you are able.

Your first surprise will come when you learn that many of the street-games of Stamboul children are the same as those you played yourself, a continent away and a generation past – so universal is this freemasonry of the young. Only the names are different; Blind-Man's Bluff is known in Stamboul as *Korebe*, Tag is *Kovalamaca*, and that old side-walk-game of Hopscotch is known here as *Sek Sek*. And It, that long-suffering character central to most children's games, is known in Stamboul as *Ebe*. Poor *Ebe* is abused, taunted, beaten and blindfolded here just as It was in the games of our childhood. Although their rituals are much the same as those we remember, many of the Stamboul street-games seem to bear more colourful names than ours; as, for example, the Prostitute's Bundle, the Fish Fled, the Velvet-Maker's Beauty, and the Golden Cradle. Then, too, the nonsense-rhymes which accompany so many Stamboul street-games seem even more lyrically silly than those of our own games. Listen to the boys shouting '*Chinko, minko, triko, puff!*' as they blow their buttons towards the goal in the game called, naturally, Puff. Or hear the girls cry out '*Anya, manya, kumpanya; bir şişe şampanya!*' as they taunt poor *Ebe* in the game known as Holding Corners. But perhaps our memory is failing us and our own children know sillier rhymes yet in English and American games.

Here, then, are summary descriptions of a few old favourite Stamboul street-games, along with their accompanying chants and nonsense-rhymes:

Hen with Eggs: *Ebe* is chosen and blindfolded. The others take a ball and hide it somewhere. When they have done so they take two stones and strike them together, chanting meanwhile, 'Hen with eggs! Hen with eggs! Where are your eggs? In the nest! In the nest!' As soon as *Ebe* hears this he takes off his blindfold and begins to search for the ball. When *Ebe* finds the ball the others run away in all directions. *Ebe* chases after them, trying to get close enough to hit someone with the ball.

While he runs *Ebe* shouts: '*Git git gidak! Git git gidak!*' – If you hear this cry echoing along the back streets of town you had best flee, or you may be hit by the ball and thereby become *Ebe* yourself!

Blind-Man's Bluff: *Ebe* is chosen and blindfolded. The children form a ring and walk around him, chanting this rhyme: 'We turn singing songs. Know who we are by the stick in your hand. Show us, blind man!' *Ebe* then touches one of the players with his stick and rubs his hand over the child's face, trying to identify him. If he succeeds the other child becomes *Ebe* in turn.

I Sell Oil: After *Ebe* is chosen the children sit in a circle, facing towards the centre. *Ebe* takes a handkerchief and marches with it around the outside of the circle, singing this song: 'I sell oil, I sell oil. My mother is dead so I sell oil.' At that point in his song *Ebe* drops the handkerchief and runs. The child behind whom the handkerchief is dropped must quickly pick it up and catch *Ebe* before he reaches home-base, which here is known as the *Kale*, or Fortress.

Open, My Lock: After *Ebe* is chosen, the other children gather round and close their fists one above the other. *Ebe* takes his index finger and inserts it into the topmost fist as if putting a key into a lock. *Ebe* then turns his finger-key and opens the fist-locks one-by-one until he comes to the last one. The following dialogue then takes place between *Ebe* and the last boy in the lock-column.

Ebe: 'Open, my lock, open!'
Last Boy: 'Lock won't open!'
Ebe: 'Where is the key?'
Last Boy: 'Fell into water!'
Ebe: 'Where is the water!'
Last Boy: 'Goat drank it!'
Ebe: 'Where is the goat?'
Last Boy: 'Fled to mountains!'
Ebe: 'Where is the mountain?'
Last Boy: 'Burned, became ashes!'
Ebe: 'Where are the ashes?'
Last Boy: 'Scattered!' (shouting)

As soon as the last boy shouts, 'Scattered!' he and all of the other boys run away in all directions. *Ebe* then strokes his chin and says, 'Oh, my hairless beard!', whereupon he chases after the other boys, trying to catch one of them.

If poor *Ebe* is too slow of wit and foot to catch anyone in these games he might seemed doomed to remain *Ebe* indefinitely. However, he does have one way out. At any point during the course of the game *Ebe* may shout '*Estepeta!*' and all players must freeze in position until *Ebe* releases them by shouting '*Boz!*' If anyone moves, speaks, smiles or giggles during this interval then that person is declared to be *Ebe* and the old *Ebe* is released from his bondage. This auxiliary game of *Estepeta* is very popular among tired *Ebe*, for silly Stamboul children are very prone to move, speak, smile or giggle during an enforced silence.

When strolling down the back streets of Stamboul you will occasionally pass through a gauntlet of waiting children. They are lined up there neither to stone nor to honour you, but are merely waiting for you to pass so that they can continue their game. These are among the most popular Stamboul games, where the players line up on opposite sides of the street and exchange sides according to some ritual accompanied by rhymes so old that their meanings are lost to the children who recite them. Perhaps if one side is short a player and you are not too old and infirm you might be asked to play. On the very unlikely chance that you will make the team, here are the directions for playing two favourite old street-games of Stamboul children:

The Velvet-Maker's Beauty: The children line up in two equal groups on opposite sides of the street. The leader of each group then secretly assigns false names to each of his players. When they have done this one team then chants the following rhyme: 'The velvet-maker's beauty is in the inn, is in the inn. *Tahtakale, kurbunde*, we will come to you in ten days!' The other team then replies: 'If you come, you come. Come and make us happy! Box is inside box. Choose the one you love!' When this song is finished the leader of the first team calls out a name. If this happens to be one of the false names assigned to one of the players on the second team, then that child passes over to the other side. If the leader fails in his first attempt he is given two more chances. The two groups then alternate in this way until one team has captured all the players of the second. This game can go on for hours, for Turkish children are endowed with a rich variety of first names. Often the game is ended only at nightfall, when the irate mothers of the players summon them home by their real names.

Regiments, Regiments: (This is a very old game, as you might guess from its archaic chorus, and it may by now have passed out of the repertoire of Stamboul children.) An even number of children divide into two rows which face each other across the street. The following dialogue then ensues between the two children at the end of the rows:

Left: 'Regiments, regiments, listen to me you regiments!'

Right: 'What do you want from our regiments?'

Left: 'I saw a beauty among you; I want her!'

Right: 'Tell us her name!'

Left: 'Her name is Ayşe!'

Right: 'Ayşe is not beautiful. Her foot is lame, eyes twitch, ears deaf, body fat, crooked shape, breasts sag, teeth stick out etc. What will you do with her?'

Left: 'I don't care if her foot is lame etc. etc.; I'll take her as my wife and give her the crown from my head!'

Right: 'Take her and let her be yours!'

The spokesman from the left line then crosses the street and escorts Ayşe to his side. The spokesman of the right row then repeats the procedure and chooses a player from the left row (using a different description of the girl's supposed deformities), until finally the two rows have completely interchanged players. The leaders of the two teams then hold each other's hands and the other children circle around them, singing this song: 'Regiments, regiments, listen our regiments! Come in, here are our palaces! We found our beauties here, and entered, hand and hand.'

The street-games of the younger children of Stamboul are usually quite simple; nevertheless they are always charming and the nonsense rhymes which accompany them have often an innocent lyricism. Here are a few old games for younger children which may still be seen and heard in the quieter back lanes of Stamboul:

Sing, My Bird: A group of girls sit in a circle around *Ebe*, whose eyes are blindfolded. *Ebe* has a small cushion in her hand which she places in the lap of one of the girls and says: 'Sing, my bird, sing!' The girl then sings a song, attempting to disguise her voice. If *Ebe* identifies the voice of the singer then that girl herself becomes *Ebe*.

Fish, Fish, *Kayıkçı*: (A *kayıkçı* is a boatman, usually a fisherman.) Two children sit facing one another. They put the soles of their feet together, hold one another's hands, and then rock back and forth as if rowing. While they row they sing this song: 'Fish, fish, *kayıkçı*. Swish, swish goes the oar of the boatman, and tap, tap goes his heart. I have meat at my house, and also a mischievous cat. If the cat eats the meat and my mother beats me, then fish, fish, *kayıkçı*.'

And for two small girls minding their baby sister there is always the old game called Golden Cradle to pass the time away. The two girls sit facing each other and cross their hands so as to form a cradle between them. The baby is then placed in this arm-cradle and rocked back and forth while the girls sing this song: 'Who swings in the golden cradle? The baby in the flamboyant clothes!'

A tinsmith's shop on the Street of Caldron-Makers

13

The Dust of Seven Shops

The Fourth Section of the Procession of the Guilds was headed by the Chief Physician of the Saray, and Evliya tells us that he was followed by one thousand doctors of medicine. According to Evliya: 'At the public procession they adorn their litter with all the instruments of their profession, with clysters, draughts, pills, etc., feel the pulse of sick men, and give medicines to them. The Prophet said, "Science is twofold, the science of bodies and the science of religions." The science of medicine is very old, and in the earliest time it was patronised by Pythagoras the Unitarian, and by the divine Plato, Hippocrates, Socrates, Aristotle and Galen, who split a hair into forty parts, and raised a ladder for science to ascend to heaven; but finding no remedy against death, they were obliged to leave this world.'

The Physicians were followed in the Procession by the Oculists, eighty in number. As Evliya tells us: 'Their first patron was a Jewess of the time of Moses, who was directed by God to apply to her for relief for his sore eyes. This woman took dust from under the right eye of Moses and put it into his eye, by which means he was cured. The patron of Oculists in the Prophet's time is buried in Isfahan, and the dust of his tomb is reckoned as a specific against sore eyes. The Oculists make a show upon litters of all their unguents, medicines and instruments, giving physic to men with diseases of the eye.'

And the Oculists were followed in turn by the Merchants of Collyrium, the Confectioners of Electuaries, the Apothecaries, and the Surgeons, who 'parade at public processions with litters full of instruments to draw teeth, as well as saws, lancets, and other instruments of surgery. They pass with jests as if they were dressing wounded heads, broken arms or feet.'

Although modern science has come to Stamboul since Evliya's time, many of the conservative Anatolians who live here still swear by more traditional medicine. In the poorer quarters of the town the sick often have recourse to folk-healers called *büyücü*, who make use of cures and remedies reminiscent of those which Evliya describes. And since, as Evliya wrote, science is twofold, many of the complaints from which the poor seek relief are not physical but psychic or spiritual, which is to say that the *büyücü* serves as a folk-magician as well as a quack salver.

Many of the most common maladies from which the superstitious of Stamboul suffer are thought to be brought on by *nazar*, or the evil-eye. *Nazar* is not such a serious problem as it was in the old days, but there are still a few ancient, snake-haired witches who may dart their malevolent glances at you as you pass beneath their windows. If you have the misfortune to fall under the spell of one of these wrinkled crones, forget about modern medicine and psychiatry, and, instead, place yourself in the care of your neighbourhood *büyücü*.

The *büyücü* agrees with more conventional practitioners of medicine in advising sensible precautionary measures. To ward off the evil-eye wear a blue-eyed bead called the *nazar boncuğu*. Young children are especially susceptible to the evil-eye, and so when admiring them be sure to say '*Maşallah!*' (What wonders God hath willed!). (The ram-shackle folk-buses of Stamboul must constantly be in danger from the evil-eye, for they are all festooned with *nazar boncukları* and other protective amulets, and all bear the pious slogan '*Maşallah!*' But alas! from the number of wrecked buses one sees around town, it would appear that even the most potent talismans are ineffective in Stamboul traffic.) It is also advisable to avoid the known haunts of evil spirits, such as graveyards, ruined houses, abandoned hamams, and junkyards. Above all, never urinate or defecate in those places for that is sure to infuriate the resident ghosts. If your business takes you to such spooky places, arm yourself with protective beads and amulets and repeat propitiatory expressions such as '*Bismillah!*' (In the name of Good) and '*İyi saatte olsunlar!*' (Let them be at a good time). And one last warning: avoid the glance of blue-eyed people, for they are most likely to have the power of the evil-eye. (If you are blue-eyed yourself, you may find peasants avoiding *your* glance in certain backward sections of Stamboul.)

But even if you are stricken by the evil-eye all hope is not lost, for your local *büyücü* may still be able to rid you of the spell. In one of the most effective treatments for evil-eye infection, the patient is fumigated while the *büyücü* pronounces the following incantation: 'White eye, black eye, blue eye, green eye, yellow eye, brown eye; whichever was the evil-eye disturb and overthrow its magic!'

Some of the wizard fuels used to generate this sorcerer's smoke are listed below:

Small pieces of wood cut secretly from the victim's house.
Pieces of hair, clothes and old shoes taken secretly from the victim.
Salt, pepper, onions and garlic wrapped together in blue paper.

It is quite possible that in his course of treatment for ridding one of the evil-eye the *büyücü* may recommend other remedies. Some of the most effective (and most bizarre) of these are the following:

Wash thoroughly with water whose weight is equal to that of seven
  Korans.
Perform the ritual ablutions with water from a mill-wheel.
Drink a potion of porcupine blood.
Inhale the fumes from a burning snakeskin.
Wash with water in which twigs from a stork's nest have been boiled.
Take the excreta of a swallow, dissolve it in coffee and drink. (Some
  Stamboul coffee always tastes this way.)
Take the dust of seven shops, mix with stork droppings, sprinkle
  with caraway seeds, burn and inhale.
Take the dust of seven shops, a strand of a spider's web, a fragment of
  a bat's wing, shred a beet stolen from a neighbour, mix well and
  dissolve in water, then wash with the solution under an archway.

The *büyücü* of Stamboul have also a vast library of magical inscriptions to be used for various purposes. These formulae are written by the *büyücü* in Arabic script and are to be used in certain prescribed ways. A few of these prescriptions are listed below (given without the pertinent Arabic inscriptions, of course, since if these were written down, even in a serious essay like this, they might still work their magical purposes and so cause unpredictable mischief).

> To punish theft: Write the proper inscription on an egg and put it into the hottest part of the fire. This will cause the feet of the thief to break and his sight to fail, reducing him to the level of a beggar and depriving him of the benefit of what he stole.
>
> To bring milk to a woman: Write the proper inscription on her breasts.
>
> To find a husband for a spinster: Write the proper inscription on the lady's navel. (The *büyücü* were often accused of serving their own immoral purposes with such inscriptions, but the homeliest girls of old Stamboul had to take whatever help was at hand.)
>
> To bring back an escaped husband: On the door of the house write '*Beddua*', which is a malediction. Also write the proper formula on a walnut shell and place it in the escapee's bed.
>
> To induce pregnancy: Write the proper inscription on a piece of blue paper and place in the woman's bed. (Presumably the lady's husband has to play his part as well, if he is able.)

The *büyücü* is also qualified to perform black magic for malevolent purposes. The fees are somewhat higher in these cases because of the risk which the *büyücü* takes in the event that his practices are discovered by the irate victim.

> To separate a couple: Rub pig-oil on the victims. Or, on a Sunday evening write the proper inscription on two pieces of bread and give one to a dog and the other to a cat. If the animals fight one another, so much the better.
>
> To bring someone under your control: Cause the victim to eat the tongue of a donkey treated by the *büyücü*.
>
> To sow discord in a house: Kill a snake and throw it into water, leaving it there for three days. Pour the snake-water on the threshold of the house where discord is desired.

Firewood merchant and a local boy

To make someone ill: Take a piece of soap, write the victim's name on it, stick a needle into each letter, and throw it into a dried-up well.

To get someone into difficulty: Buy the shoulder-blade of a cow, write the victim's name on it, and hang it from the branches of a dead tree. (For this reason the honest butchers of old Stamboul would never sell this baleful bone but smashed it instead.)

The *büyücü* of Stamboul also possess a bizarre but effective pharmacopoeia of folk-medicines. Some of the most highly recommended remedies are the following:

For boils: Place a poultice of hen-droppings on the boil.

For headaches: Take three sliced lemons or potatoes and place one on forehead and one on each cheek. Or, crush horse-chestnuts, inhale, and sneeze away the headache.

For bloodshot eyes: Take the warm white of a boiled egg and place it on each eye in turn.

For eye infections: Take the milk of a woman who has just given birth to a daughter and add to it garlic-powder and bay leaf and drop into eyes.

For constipation: Take the white part of a rose, boil and drink.

For stomach ache: Eat the inside of a peach-pit. Or, take a piece of bread and dip into vinegar, sprinkle with powdered dandelion leaves and place on stomach.

For earache: Take a baby mouse without fur, place in a bottle of olive-oil and wait until the mouse has dissolved. Then drop into ear.

For coughs: Put honey on your back and sprinkle with black pepper.

For falling hair: Take ashes or tar from an old pipe and place on balding head.

For hepatitis: Take camel-urine, mix with water and drink. (Some may prefer the disease to the cure.)

For warts: Go out on the roof between the fourth and fifth occasions of daily prayer and say: 'Tonight is the night of warts and stars, tomorrow where will be only stars.' Repeat this for three nights and the warts will disappear.

For a contraceptive: Let the man boil an earthworm and drink the
water. (This may put more sensitive lovers off their game entirely.)
For sterility: Take the hair of an Arab, mix with limestone and arsenic,
roll into small balls and use. (Use how? Sometimes these folk-
prescriptions are a bit vague; surely one should use this remedy
externally, but where? Perhaps on the Arab himself.)
For nightmares: Walk naked to a crossroads and there sprinkle your
head with the dust of seven shops. (If you are arrested for indecent
exposure you can always produce your *büyücü*'s prescription.)

One of the most common methods by which *büyücü* effect their
magical cures is through the ritual of lead-pouring. Lead-pourers are
invariably *büyücü kadınlar* (literally lady-magicians), old women who have
inherited their quack-practice skills through the female line. There is
also a rival guild of sherbet-pourers, who claim great influence in the
spirit-world, citing as evidence the known predilection of spirits for
sweets.

But, sorry to say, these old-fashioned practitioners of folk-medicine
are fast disappearing from the life of modern Stamboul. Soon we will be
left in the scientific hands of doctors and psychiatrists, and the neglected
ghosts of Stamboul will have to find a less enlightened town to haunt.
But with the *büyücü* nearly extinct, do not feel that you are helpless against
the evil-eye. If you are ever stricken by a sinister, witch-shot glance, you
can always gather the dust of seven shops and dose yourself.

Byzantine gate leading to the Gypsy village of Sulukule

14

The Gypsy Village

The Gypsies of Stamboul also had their place in the Imperial Procession, and Evliya describes them thus as they pass in the parade: 'The Leaders of Bears are Gypsies who have no patron; they inhabit the quarter called Shah Mahalleh in the suburb of Balat. They number about seventy men, having strange names such as Hayvanoğlu (Son of an Animal), leading bears with double chains and playing on tambourines.' Other Gypsies from this quarter marched in the Procession with the Beggars, the Dung-Searchers, the Fortune-Tellers, the Dancing Boys, and the Fools and Mimics, those lowly guilds to which they still belong today.

The quarter which Evliya called Shah Mahalleh is today known as Sulukule, the neighbourhood just inside the ancient Byzantine walls near the Edirne Gate. There has been a Gypsy encampment in this quarter since as far back as the thirteenth century, when an edict issued by the Emperor Andronicus Comnenus gave them permission to reside inside the city walls. But other edicts issued by the church and state authorities of Byzantium warned citizens to beware of Gypsy fortune-tellers, magicians, musicians and bear-leaders, by which we learn that they have been up to the same tricks since they first arrived in town.

While gold-toothed Gypsy matriarchs tell fortunes and peddle aphrodisiacs in incensed and smoky parlours, their vulpine-visaged mates are prowling the streets as itinerant tinkers, one eye always cocked and ready for some illicit enterprise; their ribald, mushroom-necklaced sisters are hawking herbs and flowers, probing junk-heaps with the trained eye of an archaeologist, giving mocking and blatantly erotic glances to every man they pass; their lean and larcenous-looking sons are leading bears and rattling tambourines; their nimble, nubile daughters

are belly-dancing in nightclubs or begging on street-corners with their
sleeping infants, looking like dark and corrupted madonnas; their
raucous, ragged grandsons are singing, scraping on fiddles, pounding on
drums and performing acrobatics in front of taverns; their barefoot,
tangle-haired granddaughters are charming pedestrians out of their
wallets . . . What would the streets of Stamboul be without them?

The Gypsy village in Sulukule was only about two hundred yards
long; just a crazy one-sided street consisting of a row of brightly painted
ramshackle houses propped up against the city walls. This was the gayest,
noisiest, dirtiest, most colourful and most disreputable street in all of
Stamboul, and although there were never more than a few hundred
people living there at any one time, they seemed to generate more
turbulent, joyous, boisterous life than the rest of the town taken together.
The safest time for a timid foreigner to visit Sulukule was in early afternoon, for then most of the more dangerous and troublesome characters
in the village would be away in town. The only ones left in the village at
that hour of day would be: young women temporarily out of action
because of advanced pregnancy or because they were waiting for things
to cool off a bit for them in Pera; young men who, like alley-cats, were
licking their wounds before foraging once again in night-town; children
too old to be carried in their begging mother's arms but not yet graduated
from their own beggar's apprenticeship; a few of the more handsome
young men and women who were waiting for their admirers to come
calling on them; gold-toothed termagants who kept house for their
children while they hustled a living in the city; and bored patriarchs
living now in comfortable retirement on the earnings of their wives
and daughters. But even with only that skeleton force of Gypsies on
hand, a foreigner could find his first visit to Sulukule quite shattering.
No sooner had you crossed the hill above the old Gate of the Assault
than advance scouts of village boys spotted you and gave the alarm to
the whole community. Card-games and *tavla*-matches stopped and the
village teahouse emptied; women ceased their gossip and stationed
themselves at doors and windows; infants, old men and senile bears
were roused from their afternoon naps; young girls smeared on fresh

lipstick and arranged their hair; beggars, both apprentices and retired ancients, began twisting their limbs into distorted shapes; while a mob of screaming children and barking pariah dogs raised a cloud of dust as they raced up the road to meet you. At this point some foreigners were apt to take to their heels and run for safety down the Street of the Little Fountain, not realising that a rearguard of Gypsy-kids was rushing the other way to cut them off. The best course of action, then, was to say a prayer, steady your nerves, hide your watch in your shoe, clutch your wallet to your breast, and hope for the best. If the foreigner was a hero and survived this first assault, his visit to Sulukule could be very enjoyable and interesting; the children satisfied their curiosity and went back to their games; the dogs resumed their dung-searching; the women picked up the thread of their interrupted gossip; the men went on with their drinking and gambling; ancients, bears and infants went back to sleep and beggars unwound their distorted limbs. And as the foreigner finally walked down the village street, the only ones who paid him any undue attention were a few octogenarian courtesans, who flashed him golden smiles and invited him into their parlours, and gave him a ribald salute when he politely declined. The foreigner could then sit himself down in the village teahouse and converse amiably with the village elders, observing from there the life of that colourful encampment.

On the occasion of my own first visit to Sulukule, I was there introduced to the King of the Gypsies, Stamboul branch, whom I had earlier observed urinating against the Byzantine city-walls. The King and I sat together in the village teahouse for some time, exchanging pleasantries and drinking rakı. Then I suddenly became aware that the village had grown unnaturally quiet. I was about to question the King about this when, quite abruptly, a door flew open in a shack across the way and a woman came storming out, shrieking at the top of her lungs and pounding on a finger-drum. A crowd of children quickly gathered around her and then the woman marched off down the middle of the village street with the children following in procession behind her. As they marched back and forth through the village, this madwoman pounded on her drum and ritually chanted phrases which were picked up and repeated by the children behind her. I asked the King what was going on and was told that this woman had had an argument with her neighbour over someone else's husband and that she was now putting a curse on said neighbour. The ritual of this curse seemed to involve a vivid enumeration of the neighbour's sins, which were legion, judging from the number of chants which were intoned. The march finally ended when the madwoman stalked over to the village fountain and stood there with one foot on the tap, shrieking one last curse while she pounded furiously on her finger-drum. There was a brief moment of silence followed by a wild cry of rage from a shack beside the teahouse. I needed nobody to interpret this sound for me – war had been declared. The village was absolutely quiet again for a few seconds and all activity ceased. Then the accursed Gypsy emerged from her own shack and faced her adversary at the fountain, and the two began striding down the street towards one another, black eyes flashing, white teeth bared, red nails unsheathed. They collided like spangled alley-cats and began rolling around on the ground in a snarling, spitting, hissing tangle of bracelets, beads, skirts and bandanas, screaming in rage and pain as they pulled out tufts of dyed hair and raked one another's rouged cheeks with their red talons. After a few minutes of this the King directed that they be separated and they were dragged back to their respective shacks, from where they continued a verbal barrage across the street for a while and then finally fell silent. The King was quite disgusted. He told me that such fights were often staged in the evening for tourists; but for these two hell-cats to have torn one another's eyes out in the middle of the afternoon with no paying customers about – it was completely senseless, and, besides, it disturbed his *keyif*. The King then sighed and remarked to me that he was tired of just hanging around and looking after this village of quarrelling women, while everyone else was having fun and making money in town. He would re-tune his saz, he said, and begin playing once again in the cafés in Beyoğlu. The King and I had a last rakı together on that happy thought.

But that is all in the past, for just last year the police drove the Gypsies from Sulukule and smashed their shacks to pieces. Today if you walk

along the city-walls near the Edirne Gate you will no longer be set upon
by mobs of spirited Gypsy gamins nor will you be accosted by obscene
old women wearing golden coins on their ears. Sulukule is now as quiet
and lifeless as the cemeteries outside the walls. The only signs that the
Gypsies were ever there are the poignant, house-shaped patches of
bright blue and pink and orange paint along the ancient city-walls,
marking where the Gypsy shacks once stood. After all these centuries of
colourful and uninhibited life the Gypsy village of Sulukule is now gone;
vanished, as the saying goes, 'like a Gypsy grave'. I suggest that a plaque
be placed high on the Byzantine defence-tower in Sulukule and that it
be inscribed with these words of Evliya Efendi, commemorating the
Gypsies of his day and of our own: 'There are also some Gypsy jugglers
called *hezarcıyan* (skilled in a thousand arts), who would be able to give
lessons to the devil, to put fleas into cages and lice before a wagon, to fly
with eagle's wings from the Galata Tower to Üsküdar, and, in short, to
perform incredible things.' The Gypsies of Sulukule could do all those
things and more, in their day.

An Assyrian woman and her cat

15

The Hunger of Elephants

In Evliya's time, the only animals which were believed to have been admitted to paradise were these: Katmir, the dog of the Seven Sleepers of Ephesus, Jonah's whale, Ishmael's ram, Abraham's calf, the Queen of Sheba's ass, the ox of Moses and Mohammed's camel. Tradition tells us that the heavenly gates have also opened for a bird, the cuckoo of Belkis, and for a single lucky insect, the ant of Solomon. We are surprised, at first, to learn that there is no sainted cat among the blessed creatures in the heavenly zoo. After all, if even the lowly ant, the monstrous whale and the dumb ox have gained entrance to heaven, then why not the cat, which is surely better suited than they are to enjoy paradisical pleasures. But then we realise that cats have already found an earthly paradise here in our town – just listen to them purring along the cobbled streets of Stamboul!

The cats of Stamboul are far more eastern in their ways than are the erect residents of the town. See them slinking down the streets, looking warily around them with hooded eyes, radar-ears pricking at the suspicion of an enemy's tread, ready to spring into action should an illicit opportunity reveal itself, watchful always for the chance to rape or plunder, graceful in their stride and sleek in their dress, these criminal aristocrats of the alleyways, corrupt from their claw-scarred noses to their bitten-off tails, oriental from the glittering agate eyes in their Egyptian heads down to their lethal, cobble-wise claws.

Observe these eastern cats quarrelling over entrails and fish-heads beneath the stalls in the fish-market, where their ancestors have fought and dined for centuries. See them poised on the drainpipes and ledges in the Passage of Flowers, waiting to pounce on a fat and unwary, waddling rat. Notice them couchant and contemplative on the sun-warmed cobbles in the afternoon, tawny sphinxes waiting for a handout. Later, watch them as they awake and stretch themselves languorously, and then head for dark and odorous alleys in search of food and sex, serenading us through the night with cries of love and battle. These wise cats know the cobbled streets of Stamboul better than do we, for they are closer to them.

Even in the poorest parts of Stamboul the street-cats are often as fat and sleek as pashas. This is usually due to the bounty of some local cat-lover, many of whom do not look too well-fed themselves. One of the best-known of these is a quaint character in our own neighbourhood known as Kedi Dede, the Grandfather of Cats. He is an ancient Armenian gentleman with a long white, tobacco-stained beard, long white hair which hangs down over his shoulders, and the solemn face of a broken-down prophet. His only garment is a threadbare wreck of an overcoat which trails behind him in a ragged train, and he is shod in whatever fragmentary wrecks of shoes he finds abandoned on the cobbles. He is also known as Afaroz, or the Excommunicate, from the fact that he was many years ago excommunicated from the Armenian Gregorian Church. No one now living remembers what brought about his excommunication, but, whatever it was, he is still a total outcast from the Armenian community and, for that matter, from all other communities. But, although an outcast, his dignity and simple kindness have made him one of the best-loved figures in town; in fact the ordinary people of Stamboul believe this excommunicate to be a saint. Wherever he goes he is surrounded by cats, for he is their principal benefactor in town. I sometimes see him in the Passage of Flowers or in the fish-market beside the Galata Bridge, searching for scraps with which to feed his dependent cats. He must spare very little for himself, for he is but a frail shadow of a man. Up until a few years ago he lived with his cats in the basement of a Greek church in the village of Bebek. But eventually his family of cats grew so large that it began to interfere with the normal functioning of the church. The village priest then told the old man that either he or his cats would have to go. And so, one day, we saw Kedi Dede walking sadly down the Bosphorus road from Bebek to Rumeli Hisar, surrounded by his displaced cats, looking for a new home for them and for himself. They lived for a while in a ruined, roofless mosque near the seashore; but soon Kedi Dede's health began to fail and he seemed barely able to drag himself along, supporting himself with a splintered tree-branch. Finally he disappeared from sight altogether and no one saw him for several months. We all remarked that the cats in our village seemed thinner and more neglected since his departure. Then one day I met him again in a crowded public-taxi returning from town. In my broken Turkish I asked him where he had been all that time and about the state of his health. To my great surprise he answered in perfect English and told me that he had been in the hospital with pneumonia. He was now fully recovered, he reassured me, and was looking forward to his homecoming. Then he asked me about myself, saying that he had often seen me wandering down the back streets of Stamboul and always wondered who I was. I told him that I was a teacher in the American College in Bebek. He smiled and said, 'Ah yes, the American College; I graduated from there myself fifty years ago. It is an excellent place of which I have many happy memories.' For the remainder of the taxi-ride we talked about the fascinating political manoeuvrings then taking place in the synods of the Armenian Gregorian Church and other such matters. When the taxi finally stopped in Rumeli Hisar, I was not at all surprised to see a large crowd of mewing cats waiting for my sainted companion. Such is the earthly paradise enjoyed by the cats of Stamboul.

And as the cats are the street-aristocrats of Stamboul, so are the dogs its wretched rabble. Mean and mangy, sick and covered with pus-filled sores, raw bones protruding through matted fur, they limp along the cobbles like hordes of medieval lepers doomed to walk for ever on all fours, crookedly. They swarm in the streets of the slums, snarling fiercely but too bootwise cowardly to risk attack. They prowl the filthy gutters, probing with their noses along the cobbles, looking for a decayed scrap or a half-gnawed bone; but to no avail, for the quicker, smarter cats have already gleaned the street and now sit in doorways smirking cynically. Occasionally a young pup will attempt to dispute with an old tom over the proprietary rights to a stinking mound of garbage. The penalty for this folly is a lacerated snout, and the educated pup returns to his starving pack, his tail between his legs and his head hung down in the immemorial hangdog attitude. And so the dogs of Stamboul can only complain and they din the nights with their howling, yowling, yipping, yelping, barking and baying, disturbing sleepless Stamboullus and dissipating the small store of good will they still possess in town. Occasionally the citizens of Stamboul lose their patience altogether and round up the packs of wild dogs which infest their streets. This happens only once or twice a century, for Stamboullus are very patient and slow to anger. Even then they do not execute the dogs, for our citizens exhibit a truly legendary kindness towards animals. Instead, the dogs are exiled to Sivriada, a tiny, barren island in the Marmara, and allowed to starve to death there. The last such canine roundup occurred in the year 1908. There are still a few ancients who will tell you of the terrible yowling that sounded across the Marmara for several nights before the last ravenous dogs tore each other apart and the echoes of the last whines died out. Stamboul slept soundly then for a few months, but eventually a few faint yips began to be heard as pet puppies emerged from hiding and in a few years the town had once again its normal canine population – ten barks for every pair of human ears.

My own dog, Lobo, who has been licking my feet while I write these lines, has just perked up his ears. What has alarmed him? It cannot be a burglar, for Lobo is quite fond of thieves and never troubles them at their work. He is enraged only by postmen and delivery boys, and there are none of them about at this late hour. No, I can hear now what troubles Lobo – it is the dog-pack in the village of Rumeli Hisar responding to their Asian cousins across the straits in Anadolu Hisar. The evening call to prayer has just finished echoing across the Bosphorus, the faithful are preparing to take to their beds, and the dogs of Europe and Asia are assembling their nocturnal choirs to serenade them.

But despite their occasional impatience with street-dogs, Turks are generally fond of animals and treat them better than is the case in some more prosperous countries. Observe the rough crowd outside the mosque in Rumeli Hisar trying to help a stricken old horse to his feet after he has fallen before his wagon, and then, failing, patting the poor dead nag and comforting his weeping owner. Walk through the sordid slums in the hills above the Golden Horn and see a group of ragged boys sadly burying their pet dog in a flower-covered grave. And if you are upset by the sight of those two Gypsies beating that old donkey, just notice the clouds of dust emanating from his worn hide. Why, they are not beating him at all, you eventually decide, but just giving him a thorough dusting! Although children and animals are often neglected in Stamboul, they are nevertheless treated with affection – another of those curious contradictions in which this town abounds.

Nowhere is this affectionate neglect of animals more apparent than in the Istanbul zoo. The zoo is located in a corner of Gülhane, the Park of the Rose House, which lies just under the walls of the Old Seraglio. This is probably the oldest zoo in Europe, for the Ottoman sultans kept a menagerie here as far back as the time of Mehmet the Conqueror, as did the Byzantine emperors before them. The Istanbul zoo, unfortunately, has fallen on bad times since the transfer of the capital to Ankara, and there is little money available for the purchase of new animals or even for the care of the old ones whose ill-fortune it is to be caged-up there. These animals, incidentally, include types not usually seen in Western zoos, such as, for example, the common barnyard pig, an object of particular fascination in a Moslem country. When we look upon the filthy, degenerate-looking sows in the Istanbul zoo we can agree with the dictate of the Prophet, who declared these porcine slobs unclean and therefore unfit to eat. And so the pigs in the Istanbul zoo provide both entertainment and an illustration of the wisdom of religious dietary laws for those peasants who look upon them with fascination and disgust.

It is no wonder, then, that the animals, birds and reptiles in the Istanbul zoo are in such a sad state, thin and dispirited, dull of eye and worn and drab of pelt, scales and feathers, their pens and cages filled with reeking mountains of dung and droppings. Only the monkeys seem to have retained their high spirits, and still amuse the crowds on Sunday with their comic acrobatics and shock them with their bawdy mannerisms. Nevertheless, the animals are treated kindly by their keepers, who look none too well taken care of themselves. The animals are not given the usual names by which they are known in Western zoos, but their keepers here call them by familiar Turkish nicknames. If you think it strange that a bear should be called *arslan*, or lion, it is just that this sobriquet is applied to brave and strong young men by their affectionate friends, and so it is that the brave and strong young bear is called a lion by his affectionate keeper. 'Come, my lion,' he says as he brings the bear his dinner, but the bear, seeing the poor fare before him, looks as if he would rather eat his keeper. For all of the animals in the Istanbul zoo, whatever may have been their exotic diet in their native habitat, are fed solely on stale, ground-up *simit*, a kind of pretzel. Now there are moments when I myself enjoy nothing better than a fresh, crisp *simit*, but the thought of a steady diet of *simit*, and stale, ground-up ones at that, would make me want to eat my keeper, especially if I had the appetite of a brave and strong, lion-like bear.

And if I had the appetite of an elephant my rage would be truly mammoth when presented with a lunch more suitable for an anaemic mouse. My son and I were strolling through the Istanbul zoo one day, when we heard the elephant trumpeting in rage and saw him rocking his cage as if determined to break it to pieces. His poor keeper was distressed almost to the point of tears and kept approaching his enormous pet with a bucket of ground-up *simit*, trying to get him to eat. 'My son, my son,' he cried, despairingly, 'why will you not eat your dinner? You must eat or you will become ill. My son, my son, please eat!' I approached the keeper and suggested to him that the elephant might not care for stale, ground-up *simit*. The keeper agreed, saying that he could readily understand this, but he was only following the director's orders. I reported this situation to a zoologist friend of mine, who thereupon went to see the director of the zoo to find out if anything could be done for the starving elephant. The director was very interested and sympathetic and explained that he himself had only recently been appointed to this position and as yet knew very little about animals. He would be very grateful, he said, if he could be advised as to the proper diet for the animals, particularly the elephant, since he was the principal attraction in the zoo. 'Tell me, sir,' said the director, holding his pad and pencil ready, 'what *do* elephants eat?'

And so it came about that the starving elephant in the Istanbul zoo was restored to a proper diet and now no longer trumpets in rage and rocks his cage at mealtime. Now his keeper smiles happily while he watches his huge pet devouring enough food at one sitting to keep him and his own hungry family well-fed for weeks. 'My son, my son,' says the keeper to his elephant, 'you will soon look like a lion once again!'

And since then, whenever I feel famished between meals, I always think of the Istanbul zoo and reflect upon the hunger of elephants.

Tombstones in the cemetery at Eyüp

16

Laughing Tombstones

Evliya Efendi begins the second part of the first volume of his *Seyahat-name* with a description of the cemeteries and mausoleums of Istanbul. The most famous cemetery in the city in Evliya's time, and still today, was that in Eyüp, a suburban village some distance up the Golden Horn. And so the longest and most interesting in this part of Evliya's work is his Description of the Sepulchral Monuments of Eyüp.

The cemetery of Eyüp is thought to be especially sanctified because of its association with Eyüp, Companion of the Prophet. According to tradition, Eba Eyüp, who was one of the leaders of the first Arab siege of Constantinople from 644 till 678, was killed in action and was buried somewhere outside the walls of the city. As Evliya tells us: 'A truce having been concluded with the Emperor on the condition that Eyüp should be allowed to make the pilgrimage to Aya Sofya and to perform his devotions there, he was killed on his return before the Crooked Gate, by a stone cast down on him by the infidels. There is, however, a tradition that he died of a disorder of the bowels.'

Evliya then goes on to tell us of the miraculous discovery of Eyüp's grave during the final Turkish siege of Constantinople in 1453:

Sultan Mehmet II, having laid siege to Constantinople, was with his seventy saintly attendants, seven whole days searching for Eyüp's grave. At last Akşemsettin exclaimed, 'Good news, my Prince, of Eyüp's tomb.' Thus saying he began to pray and fell asleep. Some interpreted this sleep as a veil cast by shame over his ignorance of the location of the tomb; but after some time he raised his head, his eyes became bloodshot, sweat ran from his forehead, and he said to the

Sultan, 'Eyüp's tomb is on the very spot where I spread the carpet for prayer.' Upon hearing this, three of the attendants together with the Sheikh and the Sultan began to dig up the ground, and at a depth of three yards they found a square stone of verd antique on which was written in Cufic letters: 'This is the tomb of Eyüp.' They lifted up the stone and found beneath it the body of Eyüp wrapped up in a saffron-coloured shroud, with a brazen play-ball in his hand, fresh and well-preserved. They replaced the stone, formed a little mound of the earth they had dug up, and laid the foundation of the mausoleum amidst the prayers of the entire army.

Many of the great men and women of the Ottoman Empire are buried in the vicinity of Eyüp's tomb. While strolling through this posh suburb of the dead we pass the tombs of historic figures: the conqueror of an empire, the governor of a kingdom, the beloved favourite of a sultan. Evliya Efendi tells us of some of the famous personages who were buried there in his day:

Kara Mustafa Paşa, the conqueror of Cyprus, is buried beneath a cupola on the left side of the courtyard of Eyüp near the interior gate; his victorious bow and arrow are suspended at his head. Gazi Pellah Mustafa Paşa, Süleyman's Vezir and Captain Paşa, who took to the sea in forty galleys and sailed around the cape to the Arabian Gulf, from whence he proceeded to Basra and was present at its siege and conquest . . . Sokullu Mehmet Paşa, the Grand Vezir of the Ottoman Empire during the reigns of Süleyman, Selim II and Murat II, who, after being at the head of affairs for forty years, was killed in the Divan by a mad soldier from the frontier in the year AH 987 (AD 1579). Amongst the monuments of the vezirs there are none greater than his . . . Musa Çelebi, the favourite companion of Murat IV; he was given up by Recep Paşa to the rebel Sipahis and his body torn to pieces at the palace of İbrahim Paşa. Sultan Murat assisted at his funeral prayer and his body was entombed at Eyüp within an iron enclosure looking on to the main road. The chronogram is written on gold letters on an azure ground.

Evliya Efendi also tells us of the divines, poets, scholars and sainted men who were buried in Eyüp in his time:

Abu Saud Efendi, the most learned divine since the days of the Prophet and called therefore a second Na'man. His commentaries on the Koran extend to twenty-four sciences and are extracted from 1700 other commentaries and have therefore no equal. He was Sultan Süleyman's *mufti*. Following the doctrines of external worship, he railed at the mystics, but finally Gülşeni, the great mystic, in the presence of Sultan Süleyman, succeeded in convincing him and obtaining from him his *fetva*, declaring the dances of the dervishes to be legal . . . Hüseyin Bukari, the son of Timur, known as the wonder of his time. He threw himself at the feet of Murat IV at Tabriz, came with him to Constantinople, died of the plague, and is buried in the courtyard of the mosque . . . Molla Sheikh Mehmet Efendi, the son of the *hoca* of Sultan Murat IV, who died in AH1011 (AD1611). He was profoundly learned in all kinds of sciences and was a remarkably good poet . . . Mufti Hamit Efendi is also buried at Eyüp; he founded a mosque and medrese in Constantinople at the place called Elephant Heights. I, the humble Evliya, for seven years frequented the general lectures in this college under Akful Efendi . . . Mevlana Seyyit Kasım Ghuberi; an excellent sweet-tongued gentleman whose conversations exhilarated many melancholy faces . . .

To appreciate the true spirit of a Turkish graveyard, we must leave the grand mausoleums around the shrine of Eyüp and follow the cypress-shadowed paths which lead up into the hills above the Golden Horn. The older Osmanlı tombstones here are beautifully sculpted and carved and are crowned with representations of the headdresses of the deceased, from which we learn their sex and station. The tombstones of the men are topped with stone turbans, tucked, folded and adorned with stone plumes and badges of rank. Here and there we see the stone turban of a Grand Vezir, an Ağa of the janissaries, a Sipahi, a Chief Black Eunuch. Those of the women are decorated with floral designs in low relief and adorned with archaic hats reminiscent of the *Arabian*

Nights, or draped with simple shawls, altogether feminine although their fabric is stone. The face of the tombstone invariably bears an inscription which tells us about the deceased; their dates of birth and death, the circumstances of their life, and, perhaps, a brief glimpse of what they were really like when alive. Few of these epitaphs are gloomy and most exhibit a stoic and very Moslem acceptance of death. Some inscriptions are actually cheerful, and a happy few even manage to laugh at death. That distinguished scholar and dean of Turkish letters, Cevat Şakir Kabaağaç, the Fisherman of Halicarnassus, has collected many of these old Turkish funerary inscriptions. These are some of the light-hearted epitaphs from what the Fisherman calls the Laughing Tombstones:

A pity to good-hearted small Efendi, whose death caused great sadness among his friends. Having caught the illness of love at the age of seventy, he took the bits between his teeth and dashed full gallop to paradise.

Stopping his ears with his fingers, judge Mehmet hied off from this beautiful world, leaving his wife's cackling and his mother-in-law's gabbling.

[On a wayside tomb]: Oh passer-by, spare me your prayers, but please don't steal my tombstone!

I could have died as well without a doctor than with the quack that friends set upon me.

I have swerved away from you for a long time. But in soil, air, cloud, rain, plant, flower, butterfly or bird, I am always with you.

[On a tombstone with the relief of three trees, an almond, a cypress and a peach tree]: I've planted these trees so that people might know my fate. I loved an almond-eyed, cypress-tall maiden, and bade fare-well to this beautiful world without savouring her peaches.

Even without the testimony of these laughing tombstones, we would

Disused Ottoman gravestone (upside down) in Karacaahmet Cemetery

find the cemeteries of Stamboul to be most pleasant and cheerful places. In good weather Stamboullus like nothing better than to pack a picnic lunch and stroll out into the cemeteries outside the city-walls, there to enjoy their *keyif* in the company of their ancestors. Eyüp is particularly popular, and late on a spring or summer afternoon there is no more felicitous spot in town than the rustic café which stands on the summit of the tombstone-covered hill above Eyüp. The café is named after Pierre Loti, the French novelist, who is popularly thought to have been a habitué there when he was writing his purple-prosed romances towards the end of the last century. We appreciate his choice as we sit there ourselves, tippling among the tombstones, and watch the lights twinkling on in Galata and Stamboul while the Golden Horn curves away below us, luminous in the fading pastels of twilight. As we sit there and sip our rakı, we remember that Evliya Efendi loved this spot too, and recall these lines which he wrote of Eyüp as it was there centuries ago:

> On Fridays great crowds resort to this spot, where those who will, bathe in the sea among the islets. Here the lover and the beloved mingle without restraint and take delight in embracing one another in the sea. You fancy you behold sea-angels swimming among the human angels attired in blue costumes. No more delightful bathing-place exists than that of Eyüp.

Ah, Evliya, your favourite bathing-place is now foul with sewage and the air is poisoned with the fumes of tanneries and slaughterhouses. Neither sea-angels nor humans have bathed in the Golden Horn now for many years. Nonetheless the filthy waters of the Horn still delight the eye at twilight, as seen from Pierre Loti's café in the cemetery of Eyüp.

From our necromantic café in Eyüp we can see on the opposite shore of the Golden Horn the ancient Jewish cemetery in the hills above the village of Hasköy. This is the most fascinating graveyard in Istanbul, totally different in spirit and appearance from that at Eyüp. There are no mourning cypresses here, no happy picknickers enjoying their *keyif*, no romantic shawled and turbaned tombstones. The tombstones here are plain and unsculpted, and many of them lie tumbled upon the ground, either through neglect or through the dark violence of some forgotten anti-Semitic outrage. In places the road which passes through the cemetery is paved with these tombstones, and as we walk along we try to read the inscriptions in the multiplicity of languages which these people have acquired in their centuries of wandering. But time and the tread of many feet have so worn these stones that the last sentiments they bore are now lost to us. We remember only a single stone which stood alone at the top of a hill, leaning in a gay and cockeyed attitude under a wind-bent umbrella-pine. The stone bore only the single name – EVLIYA – flanked by the carved outlines of two wine bottles, each perpetually pouring into half-empty glasses below. Could this be the tomb of our dear friend Evliya Efendi? But no, it is impossible. Evliya was not a Jew but a pious Moslem, and he was completely abstemious, or at least claimed to be, whereas the Evliya buried here advertises even in death his love of wine. But still we wonder, for Evliya Efendi often walked this way and has even left us this account of one weird evening he spent here in the Jewish graveyard:

Close to the Jewish cemetery in Hasköy there is a holy well, whose water if drunk seven times cures the quartrain ague. It is much frequented by Greeks. In the days when I, poor Evliya, was in love, I went for a walk one night in the Jewish cemetery and began to cry aloud: 'Good luck to me! Good luck to me!' In answer to my cry a spectre started up, whereat I fell, calling upon God with the words '*Ya Hafiz!*' (Oh Protector!), and went and hid inside the well, where I spent the night. In another place, please God, I will relate the strange things that befell me that night.

Albanian flower-pedlar

17

Galata

The final section of the Imperial Procession was made up of the Fools, Mimics, Distillers, and Tavern-Keepers. The lowly place of the Tavern-Keepers in the procession was a reflection of the Moslem prohibition of wine, but the large numbers by which the publicans were represented tell us that the Stamboullu enjoyed his drink as much in Evliya's day as in our own. As Evliya writes of the Tavern-Keepers: 'There are in the four jurisdictions of Constantinople one thousand places of misrule, kept by Greeks, Armenians and Jews. Though wine was prohibited by the Koran, yet as the Ottoman Empire is great and mighty there is an Inspector of Wine, whose establishment is at the Iron Gate in Galata. Whoever says Galata says taverns, because they are as numerous there as at Leghorn and Malta. The word Gumrah (Seducing from the Road) is most particularly to be applied to the taverns of Galata, because there all kinds of playing and dancing boys, mimics and fools flock together and delight themselves day and night.' And so we learn that Galata, too, has not changed since Evliya's time.

Although Galata was governed for centuries by the Genoese (who called themselves the Magnificent Community of Pera), it was never an exclusively Italian town. There was a considerable Greek population in Galata even before the Conquest, and in the century afterwards this was augmented by Turks, Greeks and Armenians from Asia Minor and by Sephardic Jews and Moors from Spain. In addition there were the hordes of seamen, merchants and adventurers who came sailing into the port from all over the Mediterranean and stayed to settle in the waterfront districts along the Golden Horn. And so, in Ottoman times Galata became one of the most heterogeneous towns in Europe and probably

the liveliest and most corrupt. We sense this from Evliya's description
of the Galatiotes of his time:

In Galata there are eighteen wards inhabited by Moslems, seventy
by Greeks, three by Franks, one by Jews, and two by Armenians.
The town is full of infidels, who number 200,000 according to the
census taken in the reign of Murat IV, whereas the Moslems are only
64,000. The different wards of the town are patrolled day and night
by watchmen to prevent disorders among the population, who are
of a rebellious disposition, on account of which they have from time
to time been chastised by the sword. The inhabitants are either
sailors, merchants or craftsmen such as joiners or caulkers. They
dress for the most part in the Algerine fashion, for a great number of
them are Arabs or Moors. The Greeks keep the taverns; most of the
Armenians are merchants or money-changers; the Jews are the go-
betweens in amorous intrigues and their youths are the worst of all
the devotees of debauchery.

It is no wonder, then, that Galata became the most colourful
and rambunctious town in the whole Mediterranean. The port quarter
was especially notorious for its tavernas, as we can see from this lively
description by Evliya Efendi:

In Galata there are two hundred taverns and wine-shops where the
infidels divert themselves with music and drinking. The taverns are
celebrated for the wines of Ancona, Saragossa, Mudanya, Smyrna
and Tenedos. The word *günaha* (temptation) is most particularly to be
applied to the taverns of Galata because there all kinds of playing and
dancing boys, mimics and fools, flock together and delight themselves
day and night. When I passed through this district I saw many bareheaded and barefooted lying drunk on the streets; some confessed
aloud the state they were in by singing such couplets as these:

I drank the ruby wine, how drunk, how drunk am I!
A prisoner of the locks, how mad, how mad am I!

Another sang:

> My foot goes to the tavern, nowhere else.
> My hand grasps tight the cup and nothing else.
> Cut short your sermon, for no ears have I,
> But for the bottle's murmur, nothing else.

But never fear, our good friend Evliya Efendi was not led astray by the licentious behaviour of the Galatiotes. For, as he hastens to assure us:

> God is my witness that not a drop did I drink at the invitation of those drunkards, but mingling amongst them I could not but become aware of their condition. I, who spent so much time in coffee-houses, *boza*-parlours and wine-taverns can call God to witness that I never drank anything in all my travels but the sweet *boza* of Constantinople. Since I was born I never tasted in my life of fermented beverages or prohibited things, neither tobacco nor coffee nor tea. I never tasted of any electuary but that of sweet lips, which I take sometimes for the relief of my chest. My father was of the same temper; but I being of a vagabond dervish nature, ready to sacrifice my soul for my friends, have spoken only for their pleasure's sake of all these prohibited beverages and electuaries.

For this you have our deepest gratitude, Evliya, dear friend!

The aftermath of drink was as serious a problem in Evliya's day as in our own, and hangovers in old Galata must have been quite homeric. Then, as now, one of the favourite remedies for those who had been struck down by wine was *işkembe çorbası*, or tripe soup. Here is Evliya Efendi's description of the tripe soup-sellers of Galata as they pass by in the procession of the guilds:

> At night many people assemble in their shops who in order to get rid of their wine eat tripe soup because, it is said, if tripe is eaten towards morning it produces that effect. At the public procession the tripe soup cooks dress cleanly, adorn their shops and wagons with china

plates, neat towels, tankards and basins, and take out of cauldrons all
kinds of intestines, which they cut up with their knives, put them into
cups, seasoning with pepper and cloves, and offer them in their usual
language, singing at the same time Greek songs. They are followed by
a train of asses carrying their intestines, which accompany their songs
by braying. They are a comical set of people.

The tripe soup-shops still line the waterfront along the Bosphorus in
Galata, ministering to the hangovers of Stamboul tipplers as they have
for centuries past.

It is clear that our friend Evliya had a great affection for the
intemperate infidels of Galata. Before he left there to wander on to
other quarters of Istanbul he paid this parting compliment to the lively
Galatiotes: 'The fair sex of this town are celebrated. The inhabitants
possess something of the nature of dervishes and in wintertime entertain
good company. The women are modest and fair.'

Ah, but they are nearly all gone now, Evliya, and Galata is not what it
was in your day. The wars and upheavals of the present century have
scattered the Galatiotes and their old town is no longer so mad and
rambunctious as it was in the past. The last to go were the Greeks, who
were raising hell in Galata up until a few years ago, but now most of
those have departed too, except for a few forlorn survivors. And so now
the streets of Galata are quiet at night for the first time in a thousand
years, and after the müezzin has proclaimed the occasion of evening
prayer the lights go out along both banks of the Golden Horn. One
evening I was sitting in an empty taverna in Galata, discussing this sad
situation with my friend, Barba Andreas the guitarist. 'Where have all
the Galatiotes gone, Barba Andreas?' I said, looking around the deserted
room. 'Eh!' he replied, 'some are dead, some have fled, and the rest have
moved to Pera.' So to Pera we went, then, Barba Andreas and I, to find
the lost Galatiotes.

We walked up though the dark, squalid alleyways of Galata, along the
Street of Nafi of the Golden Hair, the Alley of the Lonely, and the Street
of the Noble Poet. Below us we could see the light of the Galata Bridge

and of the *kayıks* and ferry boats tied up around it, but across the Golden Horn in Stamboul and below us in Galata the town was completely dark. Here and there in the dismal streets through which we passed Andreas pointed out the tavernas where he had played in the old days; Paniyoti's, Niko's, Costaki's and the Labyrinthos, where, it is said, one could hire a pirate crew to board a ship or sack a town. But now the tavernas were all silent and empty as if the Galatiotes had never sung or danced there. Soon we were up in the bright and crowded streets of Pera, among the throngs heading for the modern cafés and theatres and cinemas. I knew that those for whom we were looking would not be found in such places, and so I was pleased when Andreas turned off the main avenue and began walking downhill again into the darkness. We were on the Street of the Postmen and we were headed towards the only light in sight, a dim blue lamp which was hanging over a doorway half-below the street level. 'Hristaki's', said Andreas, and as we approached the place I could hear the twanging of a *bouzoukia* and the nasal lyrics of a Greek love song. We opened the door and walked in. The music stopped, a dozen heads turned to stare at us, and a thin little Greek halted in his solo dance, poised in mid-step with his arms spread as if he were hovering in flight, like an eagle soaring over a mountain meadow. But then they realised that the intruders were friends; they shouted greetings to us, the music resumed where it had left off, and the dancer whirled on through the remaining flights of his *zeybeki*. Hristaki and his friends asked us to sit down and have a drink with them. Andreas thanked them but explained that we were looking for some of our old friends from Galata and asked Hristaki if he knew where they were tonight. 'Eh!' said Hristaki, 'if they are not in my place they must be either in Leftero's or in Boem, for where else could one go these days.' And so we said good-night to Hristaki and his friends and left.

We walked down the Street of the Theatre through the fish-market to Leftero's. We found there a few old men playing *tavla* under the grape-arbor outside the taverna, while inside a lonely drunken Greek was singing to himself. The Greek interrupted his song long enough to tell us that life was so dull in the taverna that evening that Leftero and his friends had gone off to a livelier place. This could only be Boem, for that was the only other taverna left in town, and surely our friends would be there too. And so we walked back up through the fish-market, stopping briefly in the Passage of Flowers to have a giant draught of beer and to ask after the health of our drink-doomed friend, the Albanian Flower-Pedlar, and then on to the Taverna Boem.

The Taverna Boem is located on a little cobbled alley known as the Street of the Bright Child, just a few yards down from the main avenue in Pera. It is identified only by a dim lamp on which is written in peeling letters the simple legend, BOEM. One could spend a lifetime in this town and remain unaware of Boem's existence, passing it by like ten thousand other insignificant doorways. Since my first visit to Boem with Andreas I have spent at least a hundred evenings there, which I count among the most enjoyable hours of my life. And every time I walk through the door and push aside the old-fashioned drapes, I feel the same excitement that I did on my first visit with Andreas, for the lost Galatiotes are always to be found there; Greeks, Turks, Italians, Jews, French, Albanians and whatever other race or nationality that has found its way to this Babel of a town. The important quality of a Galatiote was never his nationality anyway, and who could be sure of that in such a swarming town as this. Whatever his race or passport, the Galatiote was always distinguished by his zest for life. And so Boem is always filled with Galatiotes.

Andreas held the drapes aside for me and I walked into Boem for the first time. Entering from the dark and silent street outside, I was not at all prepared for the sudden and almost overwhelming blast of noise which greeted me, for the whole room throbbed with the sound of laughing and singing, the clink of glasses and bottles, the roar of customers for more food and drink and the hysterical shouts of waiters trying to get it for them. The entire room and the balcony above were packed to overflowing with crowded tables of men and women and even a few children, all swaying together in disorganised and inebriated song. On the cramped little stage in the corner a four-piece band was trying to make itself heard above the din; they were just finishing the last verses of *Samiotissa*, that lovely old song of the Aegean islands. There was ancient, sad-faced Monsieur Popoff, who has been sawing away on his fiddle in this taverna for more than fifty years; gracious Madame Tashkin, who has been here nearly as long, playing her broken-down piano in this rowdy place just as if she were still on the concert stage in old St Petersburg; Costa the accordionist, who looks up and smiles as if he were sweetly dreaming in paradise; and there at the microphone, throwing his guitar up into the air as he sings the last verses of that joyous island song, is none other than the great Todori Negroponte, who for longer than anyone can remember has been the finest of all the singers and players in Galata and Pera. Todori finishes the song and then looks around and smiles at Madame Tashkin, and receives smiles himself from sad old Popoff and sweet Costa. Then they nod to each other like conspirators and begin the first mad notes of *Barba Yani*. And who are those two wild dancers who have just come out on to the floor, that dionysian acrobat with the grey moustache and flashing eyes now leaping into the air and whirling in pirouettes around the voluptuous little roly-poly lady who is undulating in a maddening belly-dance? Why it's Dimitri and Calliope and they are waving at us to join them! Calliope shouts '*Ella!*' and waves her handkerchief; the evening drinkers stagger from their tables and form in weaving line behind her as she leads them around and around the floor and up to the balcony and down again and once more around the reverberating room, while Todori throws his guitar high up into the smoke-filled air and sings yet another verse of the crazy adventures of Barba Yani. If the law allowed, they would never stop and Calliope would lead them out the door and down the avenues of Pera to their old haunts in Galata, where they would make the cobbled alleys echo with their singing as they did for so many centuries in the past. For they are the old Galatiotes, the last of that magnificent community.

Aliye Berger, the Queen of the Princes' Isles

18

The Princes' Isles

Whenever citizens of Stamboul tire of their town, or when their town tires of them, they leave or are sent to the Princes' Isles, that suburban archipelago in the Marmara. That is to say, the Princes' Isles are favoured both as pleasure-resorts and places of exile. How touching it is that Stamboullus, worn out by their rough, dirty and noisy town, and disgusted with its corrupt and perverse ways, still cannot bear to be too far away from it even when they are banished or on vacation. Observe them in one of the seaside cafés on the isles, as they sit there silent, sad and bored, looking out across the Marmara to Stamboul. Then watch them brighten up and begin to chatter gaily as the ferry arrives which will take them back to town. Observe, too, that morose and solitary character who remains at the corner table after all the rest have gone, never ceasing his gazing across the sea. The head-waiter will tell you the story of this distinguished gentleman and of how he was exiled to this island because of his crimes and intrigues in Stamboul. His crimes must have been great and his intrigues profound, for his exile is most cruel, to be banished to an isle within sight of his beloved city. But then, perhaps next year the exile will be back in town and his enemies will be packed off to the same island where he is now, perhaps to occupy the same corner table. Citizens of Stamboul have thus for centuries been travelling to and from the Princes' Isles.

Evliya Efendi made several voyages to the Princes' Isles, and has left us this lively description of one of his excursions there, the very first of his many journeys outside of Stamboul: 'All the passengers were in high spirits, and some of them implored the Lord's assistance by singing spiritual songs. Some musicians encouraged me to sing along with them, and several of the boatmen accompanied us on their instruments, with such effect that the eyes of the listeners watered with delight. Amidst these amusements we came to the Princes' Isles.' The journey today by the island ferry is usually more prosaic, but on Sunday afternoons groups of young people enliven the voyage by singing to the accompaniment of a saz or a guitar, evoking a joyous holiday mood reminiscent of that which Evliya Efendi describes.

The most beautiful of all the isles is Büyükada, the Great Island, the last one at which the ferry calls. Büyükada, as its name implies, is the largest of the isles and is also the most populous. But great, like all superlatives, is a relative term, for Büyükada is but two and one-half miles long and less than a mile wide. Islands, like planets, are worlds unto themselves and define the scale of dimensions for their exiled inhabitants.

Among Stamboullus of an older generation Büyükada is still known as Prinkipo, the Isle of the Prince, a name which was first given to it in the early centuries of Byzantium. Prinkipo has always been the most regal of the isles; its views and vistas are more sweeping and dramatic than elsewhere in the archipelago, its flora more cultivated and exuberant, its villas more elegant and their tenants more fashionable and sophisticated, its hotels grander, its cafés and restaurants more exclusive and expensive, its exiles more numerous, more illustrious and more mysterious. But Prinkipo has faded in the past generation, since the eclipse of the imperial capital on its sunset horizon. Many of the old villas are now abandoned and their windows boarded up, the grand hotels are beginning to sag a bit and seem barely able to support the corpulent pensioners who doze on their tilting balconies, and the exiles of Prinkipo have been there so long that their crimes have been forgotten in Stamboul. But one does not notice this in spring, which calls here far earlier than in Stamboul. The first harbingers of this early equinox are the flights of storks which soar up the meridians in early March across the southern horizon, to congregate for a night on İsa Tepesi, the Hill of Christos, before flying off to their summer quarters above the Golden Horn. As soon as these heraldic birds pass over

Prinkipo, some primeval signal seems given to the earth, for it erupts in blossoms and the island is transformed. The hills of Christos and St George are covered with wild flowers and adorned with flowering fruit-trees. The gardens of the old villas are set ablaze with blossoming bougainvillaea and judas trees, whose fallen petals purple the marble streets of the town. The night air becomes heavy with jasmine and honeysuckle, and under the waxing April moon the old grand hotels are seen to be festooned with heavy clusters of wistaria, whose faded lavender seems the proper adornment for those broken-down dowagers, returning to life for another season. This vernal signal also resurrects the surviving aristocrats of Prinkipo, who now pry loose the rotten boards from the windows of their ruined *konaks*, where mildewed curtains ruffle in the first hesitant zephyrs of the *meltem*. The island ferries soon resume their fair-weather schedules and begin to carry out to the islands pale Stamboullus, who stagger ashore like consumptive cripples on the quay of paradise, half-dead from a winter's purgatory in town. It is then that the moribund exiles shake the mothballs from their shiny suits and prepare to occupy their corner tables in the seaside cafés. There they will resume their eternal gazing across the Marmara to Stamboul, ceasing only to scrutinise those newly arrived off the ferry. Perhaps, one day, a retired member of the secret-police will debark and stop to chat about long-dead spies, or an old enemy will sit down to talk of past conspiracies over a glass of tea. Or, more likely, the lonely exile will just purchase the morning paper to learn the latest football score – anything to lighten the boredom which is the only cloud above this lovely island, just twelve miles from Stamboul by sea.

In modern times Prinkipo has been more popular as a place of exile than the other islands of the archipelago. After all, it is more regal and more comfortable, and an exile there can be sure to enjoy the company of more fashionable and influential people, many of them exiles them-selves, who can help him plot his way back into power. Old-timers in Prinkipo still recall two of the most fascinating exiles of a generation past, both of them foreigners. One was Leon Trotsky, who was held here as a virtual prisoner for four years after he left Russia. Trotsky lived during those years in a house not far from the ferry-landing, and there began to write his *History of the Russian Revolution*. The house in which he lived had once belonged to Arab İzzet Pasha, the head of Abdül Hamit's secret police, who himself had been exiled *from* Prinkipo after the Sultan's downfall. The second exile from that period was of quite a different type, if indeed his stay on Prinkipo can be termed an exile at all. This was Msgr Angelo Giuseppe Roncalli, later to become Pope John XXIII, who lived there during the years when he was Papal Nuncio in Istanbul. Clerical gossip has it that Roncalli was sent off there by his enemies in the Curia, who wanted that formidable personage as far away from Rome as possible. But Roncalli made the best of his exile and became a familiar and extremely popular figure in town. He is still remembered with affection on Prinkipo, and the townspeople there point out his house with pride. My dear friend Aliye Berger remembers him well, for her father's *konak* stood just beside the Nuncio's mansion. Aliye recalls that her bedroom window overlooked Roncali's garden, and that on summer evenings she would look down and see the huge figure of the Nuncio stalking through the flower beds, reciting his daily office in loud and eloquent Latin, while behind him followed a fat little friar playing upon a violin.

Not far from the Nuncio's Palace there resides another exile from the past (if indeed she is still alive at the time I write these lines). This venerable lady is the last known survivor of the harem of Sultan Abdül Hamit II, having come to Prinkipo in 1908 when the Sultan was deposed. Through all the years since then she has lived alone in a tiny house on a back street in Prinkipo. She is known only to her immediate neighbours, who see her through the curtains in her living-room perhaps only once or twice during the course of a year. Only the very oldest people on the street can remember ever having met her, many years before, but even then, they recall, her features were occulted by a heavy veil. She is known to her neighbours only as Saraylı Hanım, the Lady of the Palace.

Some of the exiles on Prinkipo found even the little island town too public and sought solitude in the wooded hills of the interior. Both of

A fisherman and his wares

the island's hills are still crowned with monasteries, where in medieval times a succession of royal exiles ended their years as monks and nuns, including several emperors and empresses of Byzantium. Today the monasteries and their churches are falling into ruins, sheltering now only one or two old monks and a few poor Greek families. The flaking plaster of the old buildings has faded into pale shades of rose and pink and the tiled roofs are overgrown with grass and wild flowers, making them the most picturesque beauty-spots on the isles – the royal exiles indeed chose felicitous hostels for their penitential years.

High on the eastern slope of Christos one sees the former residence of still another exile of former times, the Castle of Dr Hinteriyan. A castle it is indeed, complete with crenellated battlements, watchtowers, slitted turrets, barbicans, and a moat crossed by a drawbridge. But when one approaches to take a closer look one finds that the castle is a fantastic fake, constructed entirely of flimsy, unpainted wood, now rotting and falling to pieces, with yellowed newspapers flapping in its shattered windows, birds flitting through holes in its warped and rickety walls, the moat dry and filled with junk and debris. There is a rustic café in what was once the estate of the castle, and there I learned from the café owner the tale of this mad exile and his crazy castle. I was told that this medieval-looking monstrosity was built late in the last century by a certain Dr Hinteriyan, an Armenian dentist who retired here on Prinkipo after fleeing from various scandals in Stamboul. The café owner himself was only a boy at the time of Dr Hinteriyan's death, but he remembered his father telling him tales about this incredible dentist and the strange goings-on in the wooden castle during his last years. The old dentist, it seems, had fallen victim to that same mania which had seized Cervantes' hero four centuries before, for he believed himself to be a chivalrous knight errant. Consequently he built himself this medieval castle, but in wood, since time and money were short, although imagination long. And as his faithful servant, for all chivalrous knights must have a faithful servant, he hired a simple-minded Armenian fisherman named Hagop. The dentist then dressed himself and his man in medieval costumes purchased from a theatrical supply-house and set himself up as a knight in his wooden castle, ready to challenge all comers and to succour distressed damsels. But comers never came to the wooden castle, certainly not distressed damsels, and so the dentist spent all of his time carousing in the great hall, flinging empty bottles through the castle windows into the moat, while poor Hagop stood his post before the castle gate in his second-hand armour, armed with his tin sword and cardboard shield, faithfully calling off the hours of his watch and proclaiming that all was well along the walls. And so the dentist spent his last years on Prinkipo, an alcoholic knight errant in the wrong century.

I thanked the café owner for his tale and left, going back to take one last look at the wooden castle. I stood before the castle gate and observed that the moat was still filled with empty bottles, whose outdated labels commemorated the thirst of a generation past, and then I found a rusted helmet beside the ruined drawbridge. This brought the whole crazy scene back to life again, and provoked me to shout up to the castle windows. 'All is well along the walls!' I called, hoping thus to calm the ghost of that mad dentist, still haunting the creaking halls of his fake castle, still attended by the addled shade of poor Hagop.

There have been many exiles on Prinkipo besides these, but most of them have by now been long forgotten, and, in fact, the whole institution of island exile is fast going out of style. Nevertheless, there is still one old-fashioned exile in residence there. I met him one afternoon outside Villa Rıfat, which itself stands on the site of a medieval nunnery where several empresses of Byzantium were confined in their latter years, and where we ourselves are often exiled on weekends. At first I thought that this white-bearded character was an old dervish, as he trudged along the road lugging two large sacks, wearing a tattered turban on his grizzled head, garbed in a threadbare coat and shod in home-made sandals. I greeted him in Turkish and was flabbergasted when he responded in excellent but somewhat quaint English, with just the hint of an Austrian accent. I fell into step with him and soon learned the story of this last of the Prinkipo exiles. His name, he told me, was Franz Fischer, and some forty years ago he had been Professor of Microbiology at the University of Istanbul. But when the Second World War began he fled from civilisation in disgust and built himself a little shack on the uninhabited eastern end of Prinkipo, where he had lived ever since. As we walked along, various islanders greeted him as Kaya Baba, his Turkish name, and he stopped here and there to trade and sell the eggs he was carrying in one of his sacks; the other sack, he explained, contained feed for the flock of chickens and pigeons which were his only companions. By now we had become fast friends; he apologised for his poor English, which was quite perfect in pronunciation, though interspersed here and there with phrases in German, French, Latin and Turkish, saying that I was the first foreigner he had spoken to in the thirty-four years of his self-imposed exile from the world. And then he invited me to accompany him to his home, which proved to be nothing more than a chicken-coop which he shared with his birds and fowl. Through all the years of his exile, he said, the only thing he had missed was the opportunity to converse now and then with someone like myself, who could appreciate his poetry and philosophy. Whereupon he brought out from his chicken-coop two parcels wrapped in old newspapers and plastic; they contained the two tomes which he had been working on all of his life, both of them neatly printed in pencil in his own hand. The first volume was his *Aethergeist*, the Spirit of the Aether, a work of world philosophy and pantheistic theology which he proceeded to explain to me at length, ranting like an Old Testament prophet, his bright blue eyes blazing with the fanaticism of a God-intoxicated preacher. 'My philosophy is the only true one in the world, because for thirty-four years my thought has been uncontaminated by contact with the falsehoods of other books or minds!' he shouted, disturbing his pigeons so that they flew away in a flapping covey, setting his hens cackling and his cocks crowing. Whereupon he chuckled, showing me how his manuscript had become besmirched with bird-droppings across the years. 'I live with the birds, and in this way they give their opinion of my philosophy,' he said, and we laughed together till tears came to his eyes, and I realised that this must have been the first time in his long exile that he had laughed together with another human being.

When he opened the second volume his mood changed and he

became lyrical and elegiac, for this was the collected poetry of his lifetime. The poems were in chronological order, the first one written in 1917 on the Mezzolombardo front, on the eve of the battle of Caporetto. He explained that he, like Hemingway, had been seriously wounded in that battle, and that this experience had changed the course of his life. After the War he joined the Socialist Party in Vienna, had fled to Rumania when Hitler came to power, had for a time operated a delicatessen in Varna on the Black Sea coast, later emigrated to the US and found a job as butler for the Vanderbilts at their estate in Newport, and had gone to New York University at night and eventually obtained a doctorate in biology, after which he had obtained his post at the University of Istanbul. And his book contained poems from all those years and countries, written in places as far apart as a steamer on the Black Sea and a subway car in New York, all of them expressing his transcendental feeling of universal love. As I came to the end of the volume I noted that the last poem was written in 1953; it was called *Mesons and Melons* and was dedicated to Professor Werner Heisenberg, the German physicist who had formulated the Uncertainty Principle. I asked Franz why he had not written any poems after this. He paused for a moment and then answered, 'Because nothing of consequence has happened to me in the twenty years since then; I am at one with the universe and there is no longer any need to read or speak or write!' But when I said goodbye to Franz and left his little shack I could see that he looked pathetically sad, and his face lit up in a smile when I promised to return and talk with him again one day, for an exile's life can be terribly lonely even on the lovely isle of Prinkipo.

A porter carrying a heavy load over the crooked cobbles

19

Stamboul Journeys

'Allahaısmarladık!' May God keep you, I say to my friend as I take leave of him. *'Güle Güle!'* Go with laughter, he answers in the traditional fashion as he waves goodbye to me. 'Go with laughter' – now there's a fine thought for leave-taking. Does my friend wish to dispel the sadness that touches all goodbyes? Or is it that he knows there is always an element of hilarity in Turkish journeys? Something of both, I think, reflecting on my own travels in Stamboul.

The Turks were for centuries a nomadic people, and even though they have now settled down they still retain many of the characteristics of their wandering days. Most Turkish families can, if the need arises, pack up all of their belongings at a moment's notice, roll them up in the family rugs, and head off over the horizon with their women and animals in tow. Although they now move by bus instead of by camel and ox-cart as in Ottoman days, the essential atmosphere of Turkish travel has not really changed. You can still feel this nomadic quality in the outdoor bus-terminal of Sirkeci, near the Stamboul end of the Galata Bridge. But don't go there as a spectator; pack up your own belongings in an old cardboard suitcase and take your leave with the other travellers. *Güle Güle!*

The bus-terminal in Sirkeci is surely the most tumultuous spot in town. The little square which serves as the terminal and the narrow streets leading into it are crammed with ramshackle buses which only the fabled ingenuity of Stamboul mechanics has kept running on the roads. Wheezing, rattling wrecks are perpetually arriving and leaving, packed to overflowing with peasants and loaded down with the museum of belongings they have piled on top. These mechanical ruins roar in and out of the square with their horns blaring, crashing into one another, running down the struggling crowds who are fighting their way on and off other buses with their bulging suitcases and splitting bags, their bleating sheep and barking dogs, their crying children and their terrified grandparents. The foreigner feels a thrill of excitement as he hears despatchers shout the names of the ancient towns of Thrace and Asia Minor, the capitals of vanished kingdoms and lost people. But these lost peoples still live in the lands of their vanished kingdoms, and you can identify them all in the pageant of faces which passes through the terminal; turbaned and bearded Anatolians, sashed and baggy-trousered, followed by their robed, veiled and henna-handed women; a family of red-haired and blue-eyed Bulgarian refugees; a grizzled Thracian shepherd wrapped in a stinking cocoon of rags; two tribeswomen of the nomadic *Yürük*, wearing colourful archaic gowns and headdresses, rattling golden bracelets and necklaces of golden coins; a tattooed and serpent-haired *Yezidî*, or devil-worshipper, from the Syrian border; a swarthy, spear-nosed Bedouin with a gold ring dangling from his ear; moon-faced peasant girls from the troglodyte hills of Cappadocia; a giant Kurdish soldier carrying an obsolete rifle; slant-eyed mountaineers who look like the horsemen of Jengiz Khan; a little almond-eyed Seleucid princess from Antioch; blond Circassians from Trebizon with the faces of lost Crusaders; a salt-encrusted Argonaut from Halicarnassus; a pin-striped merchant from Kars with the sad eyes of a Persian poet; an Homeric tavern-keeper from Smyrna; two old men from Mardin who are either Hittite priests or Assyrian astrologers; an enormous, squat and mythically breasted Anatolian earth-mother . . . They are all Turks, or so their identity cards say, and they crowd on to your bus in one struggling mob, together with their families, their animals and all movable possessions. When the last weeping grandmother has been stuffed into the aisle, the last lost dogs and children found and put aboard, when the last battered trunk, mildewed bedding-roll, moth-eaten carpet, sack of mouldy nuts, can of bitter olives, bag of rancid cheese, brace of terrified goats and crate of angry hens has been lashed to the top, the escaped convict who is to be our driver saunters over to the bus with his arm around his handsome young assistant. They kick the bus a few times and if it does not fall apart or tip over they adjudge it fit to go. This mobile wreck is called the *Yıldırım*, or Thunderbolt, and bears above its windshield the pious legend *Maşallah!* what wonders God hath wrought! The few square inches of uncracked front window are obscured by good-luck charms to ward off the evil-eye which might be cast upon the driver by the old crones he will splash with mud along the way. Personally, I carry my own amulets to protect me from the perils presented by the coughing motor, failing brakes, shattered chassis, smashed windows and glazed tyres. Finally, after belching, scratching his behind, picking his teeth and nose and excavating the wax from his ears, our desperado of a driver starts the motor, waves to his unshaven lovers in the café, and the rattling, wheezing wreck roars at top speed through the square and out on to the highway, horns blaring, brakes screeching and wireless wailing at top volume. The perilous journey has begun and the foreigner sits in the dangerous seat of honour beside the driver as the old bus lurches down the pot-holed roads of Anatolia. Our carefree driver flirts with death at every turn, speeding around hairpin turns on mountain passes while on the wrong side of the road, jousting with other maniacally chauffeured buses for control of narrow bridges over perilous gorges. After each narrow escape from disaster the driver looks around and is applauded by his appreciative passengers, who are all enjoying the ride immensely, their heads sticking out of the windows, looking ahead for the next encounter. The faint-hearted foreigner, who is not sure if he too is under the protection of Allah, closes his eyes and reaches for his rakı bottle. *Güle Güle* indeed!

This somewhat nomadic quality attaches itself even to travel within Stamboul itself. The Stamboul proletariat travel principally on the *halk otobüsleri*, or folk-buses, those venerable mobile scrap-heaps, veterans of a thousand collisions. Your fellow passengers on the *halk otobüsü* will be the same peasants who shared with you the perils of the Anatolian roads; they survived those wild journeys and now risk their lives with you in Stamboul traffic. In recent years more modern buses have been put into service, although the rough cobbles and even rougher passengers soon reduce these to the ruinous condition of their ancestors, the folk-buses. I recall the day, many years ago, when I first saw one of these modern buses on the streets of Stamboul. 'There,' I said to a friend, 'is progress,' as we watched the bus come slowly around the corner. But then I saw that the bus was empty of passengers, and, indeed, neither was there anyone in the driver's seat. When the bus finally turned the corner I saw the reason why the driver and his passengers were all behind the bus, pushing it to a repair-shop.

The favourite mode of transport of all true Stamboullus is the *dolmuş,* or public-taxi. A *dolmuş* travels on a fixed route and the passenger pays only for the seat he occupies and according to the distance he travels. One can guess something of the quality of *dolmuş* travel by learning that the word *dolmuş* is derived from the infinitive *dolmak* which means 'to fill' or better, 'to stuff full'. That is to say, the *dolmuş* is stuffed full of people, and portly people at that, for as a wag has remarked of the Stamboullus, they represent the survival of the fattest. But Stamboullus have been stuffed into their public-taxis for so long now that the *dolmuş* have sagged and split and expanded to accommodate them, in much the same manner that a comfortable pair of old shoes give way around a pair of over-large feet. Most of these *dolmuş* are in a ludicrous state of disrepair and their drivers are among the worst on the planet. But the antiquity of these taxis and the roughness of Stamboul streets prevent them from attaining great speeds and so the accidents which befall them are often more comic than fatal. I remember once walking along the Bosphorus road near Rumeli Hisar when I suddenly saw a lone automobile tyre speeding by itself down the road. I looked around to see what had happened and then I saw about fifty yards back a three-wheeled taxi heeled over in the middle of the road, the driver and his passengers all laughing up-roariously at the sight of their escaped wheel rolling down the road ahead of them; laughing at that and at their own ridiculous predicament.

So you must choose your *dolmuş* carefully, looking cautiously at the qualities of the car and its driver, and gauge keenly your chances of survival. Pass by that swarthy, villainous scoundrel who sits sideways in the driver's seat, combing his hair with one hand while he ogles the girls he passes at ninety miles an hour. Stay out of that stolen hearse with the smoking motor, boarded-up windshield, transparent tyres and impaling seat-springs. Look over the other passengers too, so as to avoid the company of pickpockets, perverts, escaped murderers and maniacs. Take that venerable Mercedes at the end of the line, with its calm, grandfatherly driver and its cargo of retired professors and gracious Stamboullu aristocrats. They will shift over to make room for you and then the *dolmuş* will roll down the darkening streets of Beyoğlu to the Bosphorus road, with the radio jingling an old Anatolian love song as you rattle safely home over the cobbles. *Güle Güle!*

Captain Abbe, a Bosphorus fisherman

20

A Café on the Bosphorus

Evliya Efendi devotes several sections of the *Seyahatname* to descriptions of the villages and towns along the Bosphorus and of the pleasurable excursions he made to those places. In his day the shores of the Bosphorus were sparsely populated, and these communities were inhabited mostly by fishermen and their families. During the past century Istanbul has expanded out along both shores of the Bosphorus, and the seaside villages are now part of the modern city. As a result they are fast being spoiled by traffic, high-rise apartments, and by expensive nightclubs and restaurants, and so in recent years they have lost much of their former rustic charm. Nevertheless, many of the villages and their ports are still picturesque and surpassingly lovely, and here and there one catches glimpses of what life was like along the Bosphorus in Osmanlı times.

Stamboullus are generally agreed that the most beautiful stretch of the Bosphorus is about midway along its course, where it thins down to a narrow strait only seven hundred metres wide. These stretch is called Boğaz-Kesen, or Cut-Throat, for the two Turkish fortresses which stand on the opposing shores of the Bosphorus there could literally cut off the passage to enemy shipping. Anadolu Hisar, the Castle of Anatolia, was constructed in about 1390 by Sultan Beyazıt I, the Thunderbolt, who ended his days a captive in Tamurlane's cage. Rumeli Hisar, the Castle of Rumelia, was built directly across the strait in 1452 by Sultan Mehmet II, the Conqueror, thus closing the Bosphorus in preparation for the final siege of Constantinople the following year. The centuries of peace and idleness since then have softened the harsh military outlines of these fortresses, although their majestic towers and ramparts can still evoke visions of the dark and pompous beauty of medieval warfare. These old castles now seem a permanent part of the landscape, blending in with the verdant hills and valleys behind them, framed in a frieze of flowering judas trees and slender cypresses.

For those of us who have spent some years of our lives within sight of Rumeli Hisar, it is not so much an historic monument as a beloved part of the local scene. Our children have grown up under its walls and have climbed its battlements in their games. We have passed it daily on our way to work and nightly on our return from parties, and have seen it silhouetted by the sun and moon in turn when those luminaries rise over the hills of Asia. The romantics among us are moved to bad poetry at the sight of the old castle bathed in the light of a full moon, or illuminated by floodlights on holidays and holy days, its massive walls then seeming as thin and delicate as a candled egg of gold. Some of us have seen the Rose Tower reflecting the colours of a summer sunset half an hour after we thought the sun had gone, and observed the Black Tower wreathed in a sombre winter fog in a setting designed for the soliloquy of a melancholy prince. And late at night the sight of the old walls and towers brooding above the strait can make us melancholic too, when we think of the years of pleasurable exile passed in its shadows and now gone.

Those who live in the village of Rumeli Hisar are doubly fortunate, for they can look out from beauty around them to beauty on the other side, to the Sweet Waters of Asia. This is the valley formed by the two parallel streams, Göksu, the Stream of the Sky, and Küçüksu, the Little Stream, which empty into the Bosphorus a quarter-mile apart, just below the fortress of Anadolu Hisar. As Evliya Efendi wrote of the Göksu: 'It is a river resembling the stream of life, adorned on both banks with gardens and mills. It is crossed by a wooden bridge, under which pass the lovers who come here to enjoy the delicious meadows.' The fortress of Anadolu Hisar stands on the banks of the Göksu, just beyond the bridge which Evliya wrote of three centuries ago. This is surely one of the most enchanting sights on the Bosphorus, this little medieval castle nestling in among the old waterfront houses of the picturesque seaside village which has grown up around it, its archaic towers and battlements reflected in the turquoise waters of the Bosphorus, a colourful argosy of fishing boats harbouring under its mottled walls. It is no wonder that the Turks have always referred to this fortress as Güzel Hisar, or the Beautiful Castle.

And if that is not beauty enough, the Sweet Waters are flanked by still another castle on the other side of the valley, on the banks of the Küçüksu. There is nothing militant about the Castle of Küçüksu, for it was built in the middle of the last century, at a time when the frontiers were a thousand miles away and the Sultan thought less of war than of pleasure. As we stroll along the Bosphorus in late afternoon we observe the falling sun melting the glazed walls of this confectionary palace and setting on fire its jewelled windows. But then the sun sets and the palace darkens too, and we are saddened that the Sultan and his fair ladies are no longer there to keep it glowing with pleasure through the evening.

But sadness is a transitory and ephemeral feeling along the Bosphorus, and most of us spend our spare hours quite happily resting our eyes upon its beauties. Everyone has their favourite spot for Bosphorus-watching; our own is Nazmi's, a venerable waterfront café near the village of Bebek. For more than half a century Nazmi's has been a gathering place for the local fishermen and students and for the intellectuals and would-be intellectuals of Stamboul, especially those whose thought and talk require the stimulation provided by cognac and rakı in a seaside setting. And if the talk of philosophy, art and politics becomes too intense at times, and if the rival political factions sometimes shatter Nazmi's windows and splinter his chairs upon one another's heads in their drunken debates, pay them no heed, but fill your glass again, while the rising moon silvers the placid waters of Bebek Bay.

Some prefer to sit in Nazmi's by day, for then the students and intellectuals are abed, and one can enjoy the view undisturbed by their violent discussions. One will then meet the fishermen and boatmen of Bebek, who store their gear in Nazmi's back room and who sit and drink there in their off hours, which are numerous, judging from the perpetual insobriety of these salt-encrusted old characters. And so to

Nazmi's back room we will go, to learn some of the maritime lore of the Bosphorus. If you sit and drink there with old Captain Abbe he will point out to you some of the picturesque boats which sail along the Bosphorus, lineal descendants of the craft which have plied these straits since the days of Jason and the Argonauts: the *taka*, workhorse of the Bosphorus, broad of beam, peaked bow and high fantail, lumbering beauties painted in all the brightest colours of the sun's spectrum; the *mahona*, single-masted craft with lateen rig and raking stern; the *salapurga*, cousin to the *mahona* but smaller and more snub-nosed; the *bombarda*, the old-fashioned caique from the Aegean isles, often seen loaded to the gunwales with wine from the Marmara; the *martika*, the sturdy two-masted Black Sea coaster; the *karavia*, or caravel, now almost extinct, the last examples of those ships in which Columbus sailed; the *gagali*, another ancient craft, of which only one or two still remain, high poop-deck and transomed stern, bow shaped like the curve of a parrot's beak and decorated with the sign of the *oculus*, or talismanic eye, by which sailors have warded off the evils of the deep since the days of the ancient Egyptians. Captain Abbe will also point out to you with pride the boats in which the Bosphorus fishermen make their living. The most beautiful of these are the rowing *kayık*, long, slim, swift craft, each manned by about a dozen oarsmen. These *kayık* are towed in line behind powerful *mahonas*, ready to dart out across the water like sea-swallows when a school of fish is sighted by the lookout, who is pinioned like a sailor-Christ on his cross-like perch atop the lead boat.

But if Nazmi's back room is empty you should know that the *lüfer*, or bluefish, are running and that Captain Abbe, together with every other fisherman on the Bosphorus, is out in his *sandal*, or rowboat, and will not return to the café until he has caught enough to support his family for the year and to ensure his winter's supply of rakı. The *lüfer* fishing-fleet presents one of the most picturesque spectacles on the Bosphorus; each *sandal* equipped with a brilliant lamp shining down into the depths to attract the dazzled fish, together looking like a swarm of marine fireflies drifting down the dark blue stream, the night sky a lighter blue above them, crowded in luminous clusters down all the bays and coves of the Bosphorus, individual lights flitting back and forth between the invisible continents. One evening as I sat watching this extraordinary display, this yearly recurring festival of the marine-lamps which is one of the delights of our life on the Bosphorus, one of the lights detached itself from the others and headed towards the quay where I was sitting. Soon I could see that it was an old fisherman who was rowing powerfully to shore to meet his old wife, who had come down to the quay with his pailful of dinner. They conversed briefly in the yellow light of the boat-lamp and then the fisherman bade his wife good-night and rowed back out again into the dark blue stream, clouds of white sea-birds screaming around him. Soon his light had joined the others out on the Bosphorus and they drifted together slowly down the straits. Then I walked back along the quay to Nazmi's, to sit there alone and watch through the night these marine galaxies, rivalling the stars in their beauty and luminosity.

When the decimated *lüfer*-school finally completes its slow annual transit of the straits, the fishermen return to their cafés and teahouses along the Bosphorus. You might then sit yourself by the fire in Nazmi's back room and learn from Captain Abbe some of the lore of the wondrous winds and storms which trouble the straits and keep the fishermen happily idle through most of the year. That fierce wind now howling outside of Nazmi's, dashing salt spray on the windows and whistling through the cracks in the walls, is *Karayel*, the Black Wind, blowing from the cold north-eastern quarter of the compass. Later in the winter you will feel the lash of *Yıldız*, the Wind of the Thunderbolt, as it shrieks in from due north and flays any fisherman foolhardy enough to be still outdoors in that icy season. Then in January you will feel the wrath of *Poyraz*, the north-west wind named after King Boreas, mythical ruler of the obstreperous airs. *Poyraz* howls down the straits from the chill Black Sea and whitens with snow the hillsides of the Bosphorus, lays white shrouds on the moaning cypresses, powders with white the domes of seaside mosques, the roofs of *yalıs* and sea-palaces, the crenellated towers and battlements of castles, and tints the blue waters of the Bosphorus with the milk-white reflections of scudding snow-clouds. In February the wind suddenly shifts to the south east and

Keşişleme, the Wind of Mount Olympus, begins to blow moistly and the dismal winter rains begin. Cold rain pours down from lowering grey clouds for weeks on end, soaking our overcoats, filling our shoes, dripping from our beards, fogging our spectacles and our minds, drowning the town in filthy mud and discolouring the Bosphorus with ugly brown streaks. We swear then to sail away from this dark and cheerless, cloud-shrouded town and never again return, for it is doomed to a watery death and we are too, if we remain. But Captain Abbe, ordering another rakı at our expense, counsels us to be of good cheer. This alcoholic almanac then acquaints us with the windy signs and portents of approaching spring and good weather. The worst of winter is done, he says, when you feel the fresh zephyr called *Hüsün Fırtınası*, the Agreeable Storm, which wafts in across the Marmara in early March. This harbinger is soon followed by another, *Kozkavuran Fırtınası*, the Storm of Roasting Walnuts, which blows across the Bosphorus from the greening hills of Anatolia. Then in rapid succession you will see perennial vernal signs and feel the seasonal winds which accompany them. The returning birds: *Çaylak Fırtınası*, the Storm of the Kites; *Karakuş Fırtınası*, the Storm of the Blackbirds; *Kırlangıç Fırtınası*, the Storm of the Swallows; *Kuğu Fırtınası*, the Storm of the Swans; *Kukulya Fırtınası*, the Storm of the Cuckoos. Signs floral: *Filiz Kıran Fırtınası*, the Storm of Green Buds; *Çiçek Fırtınası*, the Storm of Flowers; *Kabak Meltemi*, the Pumpkin Breeze. Signs celestial: *Ülker Fırtınası*, the Storm of the Pleiades; *Gündönümü Fırtınası*, the Storm of the Summer Solstice. Then one day you will look out of Nazmi's window and see a long, stately line of storks soaring across the Bosphorus from Asia in their annual return to their ancestral nest in the cemetery of Eyüp above the Golden Horn. Now the Bosphorus becomes azure blue again, flowering judases purple the hillsides and then mature into a virginal green, giant *çınars* spread their dappled shade over Nazmi's courtyard and flowering vines carpet the café floor with blossoms. And so spring greets the local fishermen, now staggering out from Nazmi's back room, their eyes bleary from the smoke and drink of a long winter. In this season you may be troubled by the cruel beauty of nightingale-song when you stagger home in moonlight from a late party, and in your bittersweet melancholy decide that you will sleep out in the Janissary graveyard in Rumeli Hisar. You will be awakened there by the throbbing sounds of *takas* and *mahonas* labouring up the straits and feel the warmth of the sun newly risen out of Asia. You arise then and walk back to Nazmi's for a therapeutic beer and find the quay deep in brilliant blue and green and scarlet fish-nets spread out to dry in the sun. Laz fishermen and their families sit on the cobbles amid these gorgeous billows of twine and patiently mend their nets while a handsome idiot youth plays haunting melodies on a bagpipe to ease the monotony of their work. His primitive music seems to call out from their winter quarters all of the camp-followers of good weather. Soon the quay is crowded with street-boys from town, who spread out their ragged clothes to air on the cobbles while they dive and splash through the swiftly flowing garbage generated by the mobs of corpulent diners gelatinising in the waterfront restaurants. Sellers of sweet corn set up their smoking engines on the quay and vie for the penny-trade of the passers-by with pedlars of sweets, pastries, ice cream and fishing gear. The saz-player returning exhausted to his bed from the stews in Beyoğlu passes on the quay his friend, the balloon-seller, who left the same bed an hour before. Villainous Gypsies lead bears and pound tambourines, on the lookout for larceny, while across the road their dark women traffic in flowers, herbs and mushrooms, or whatever else you might desire on such a vernal day.

You might think that this fine weather would move Captain Abbe and his friends from their firm seats in Nazmi's and induce them to do some fishing in the Bosphorus; but no, they find it more profitable to rent out their *sandals* to amateur fishermen in the summer. They, the professionals, can then pocket the amateur's coin and laugh at his ineffectual attempts to catch *their* fish, while they swill rakı and enjoy their *keyif* throughout the summer undisturbed by work. Then, if you are prepared to endow him with a few more rakıs, Captain Abbe will identify for you the sweet breezes which ruffle the wistaria vines in the café, fill the sails of boats skimming across Bebek bay, and propel the fleecy clouds which float across the bright blue sky. These fair winds,

Captain Abbe says, will follow in turn on their appointed days: *Çarkdönümü Fırtınası*, the Storm of the Turning Windmills; *Kara* and *Kızıl Fırtınası*, the Storms of Black and Red Plums; and *Kestane Harası Fırtınası*, the Storm of Ripening Chestnuts. But then there may be days when you will find Captain Abbe cross and uncommunicative, and you should know that the evil wind *Lodos* is blowing from the south west, filling the Bosphorus with foul garbage and the sinus with black phlegm, shrouding the city with a miasmatic haze and irritating the entire municipality until it is an airless, sweating, seething, quarrelling Levantine hell. But never mind, keep your temper, for the *Meltem* will soon come, sweeping in from the Marmara to dispel all evil airs and harsh feelings. Captain Abbe will soon become his affable self once again and may even buy *you* a rakı, while he catalogues for you the winds of late summer and early fall, the most glorious season of all along the Bosphorus. These blow in turn as the *çınars* turn gold over Nazmi's courtyard and the grapes ripen on the trellis above your head: *Turna Geçimi Fırtınası*, the Storm of the Passing Cranes; *Meryem Anne Fırtınası*, the Storm of Mother Mary; *Bağ Bozumu Fırtınası*, the Storm of the Vintage; and *Koç Katımı Fırtınası*, the Storm of the Mating Ram. Then the skies above the Bosphorus begin to darken again, harsh winds blow down the straits from the north, and Captain Abbe and his friends begin to move out of their seats in Nazmi's – it is time to get their *sandals* ready and to work again, the fish will soon be running. You will know that the *çiroz* are back when you see these little silver fish in their tens of thousands hung out to dry from every clothesline in the city. When the *levrek* are running Captain Abbe and his mates will set out their nets in Bebek bay and then haul them in until the quay is deep in thrashing, gasping, gleaming fish, and the cobbles are covered with scales and slippery with gore. And when the word spreads that a school of *istavrit* are swimming down the straits – beware! For then every man, woman and child in town will rush to Bebek with their hooks and lines. They stand ten deep on the quay, casting their lines wildly into the water, impaling one another with their hooks, accidentally flinging their weights through the windows of passing buses, fouling their lines on passing ferries, then dashing into public-taxis when the rumour spreads that the *istavrit* school has swum on to Arnavutköy.

With the streets of our village redolent with the savoury odour of frying fish and the cats grown corpulent on fish-heads and guts, then we can all face winter cheerfully. In that mellow autumnal mood we sit under the falling leaves in Nazmi's garden, sipping our rakı to keep warm and reminiscing over the twice-picked bones of our *barbunya*, wondering if we will ever have the heart to leave this beautiful but ruinous town. Then we look out along the Bosphorus and watch the blue *mahonas* and their trailing company of *kayıks* as they set out to catch *kılıç balığı*, the swordfish, far out in the Marmara. We see them again when they return in early evening, and hear the fisherman's flute as he plays for his tipsy shipmates dancing on the fantail of the *mahona*. But all of these great fishing days begin, as Captain Abbe will tell you, only after that late October storm called *Balık Fırtınası*, the Storm of Fish.

And so the year passes in Stamboul, a cycle of seasons and their ever-recurring winds, and so we pass our idle hours and days, seated in a café beside the Bosphorus.

The grave of a holy dervish

21

The Saints in our Alleyways

In section forty-two of his *Seyahatname*, Evliya Efendi gives an account 'of the Saints and Holy Men buried in Constantinople (God be propitious to them all)'. The foreigner might be surprised to learn that this city should be noted for its sainted dead, for there are no official saints in Islam and certainly Istanbul has never been noted for its piety. But Istanbul abounds with the tombs and graves of Moslem saints, canonised only by the reverence accorded them by the pious poor of the city. The evidences of veneration are very simple; some scraps of cloth tied to a grilled window, the stumps of guttered candles atop a broken wall, a pile of stones beside an old tombstone. The tombs and graves of these saints and holy men give a kind of sanctity to the rough streets of our town.

The most popular folk-saints in Stamboul have always been called *Baba* or *Dede*; that is, Father or Grandfather. Among the poor these saints do in fact play the role of a spiritual father or grandfather. The requests made of them are often pathetically simple: to find a job or a place to live, to alleviate a pain or cool a fever, or to find a husband for a homely daughter. If you are in desperate need of work go to see Tezveren Dede on the Avenue of the Divan, for he is reputed to answer all requests quickly. To find a husband for your daughter consult Toklu Dede. His *türbe* is hard to find, for it is tucked into an enclave of the ancient Byzantine city-walls in the district of Ayvansaray – but for the plain daughters of the poor no effort can be spared. For ordinary requests you might go to Kahhar Dede at Halıcıoğlu, or to Elekli Baba at the Silivri Gate, or to Horoz Baba at Unkapanı, near the Atatürk Bridge. Horoz Baba has the simplest of *türbe*, just a small green-painted

tombstone surrounded by an iron grating on which the name Horoz
Baba is scrawled on a wooden sign. Horoz Baba, or Father Rooster,
received his name at the time of the Conquest, when he made his rounds
each morning and woke the troops of the besieging army with his
loud rooster call. Another of the Conqueror's soldiers, Yıldız Dede, or
Grandfather Star, is venerated in the district of the Garden Gate. Yıldız
Dede, as his name might suggest, was Sultan Mehmet's astrologer and
won fame by predicting the fall of Constantinople from the planetary
configurations at that time. After the Conquest Yıldız Dede built a
hamam in the district of the Garden Gate and spent the rest of his life
there in contemplation and prayer. This bath is still in use and bears the
illustrious name of the Yıldız Dede Hamam. A few ancients in this
neighbourhood refer to it as the Bath of the Jews because of the
synagogue which stood on this site before the bath was built five
centuries ago – such is the length of memories in this town. Those
who come to pray at Yıldız Dede's tomb, which is inside the bath
itself, always do so at one particular water-tap where the saint himself
practised his devotions. An inscription above the water-tap informs us
that: 'This is the place of recovery because it is the place of Yıldız
Dede.' The bath is only for men and although women are allowed in to
pray twice a month there is always a terrible commotion when they
arrive. On the floor above there is a little restaurant which serves
the best kebabs in town, the hot and spicy Arab kebabs of southern
Turkey. Synagogue, Turkish bath, Moslem shrine and Arab kebab
restaurant – this site has surely served the town well.

For one reason or another, a particular shrine may fade into obscurity
while another may become popular. A generation ago it was the custom
to take spoiled or misbehaving children to the tomb of Koyun Dede,
or Grandfather Sheep. Koyun Dede's *türbe* was in the basement of a
low wine-tavern in the Galata fish-market. The visits of female pilgrims
at Koyun Dede's tomb upset the habitués of the tavern, and the owner
barred up the entrance to the *türbe* so that it is no longer accessible. On
the other hand, the tomb of Telli Baba in Rumeli Kavak has become
extremely popular in recent years, since the opening of the new

Bosphorus highway. A special taxi-service runs from the bus-stop in Sarıyer out to the *türbe*, which is located on the summit of a hill overlooking the Bosphorus. Telli Baba's *türbe* is always gaily decorated with strands of gold and silver ribbons, left there in gratitude by the many maidens who have found husbands through his intercession. Telli Baba is said to owe some of his miraculous powers to the fact that he is in spiritual communication with Joshua the Prophet, whose own apocryphal grave is located on a hill just across the Bosphorus.

Many of the city's saints are heroic warriors who were killed during the Arab assaults on Constantinople during the seventh century. One of these is Abu Sofyan, whose tomb is in Yeraltı Cami, the Underground Mosque, which is located near the waterfront in Galata. The Underground Mosque is thought to occupy the dungeon of what was once the Castle of Galata, destroyed at about the time of the Turkish Conquest. When we descend into the mosque from the street above we do indeed have the feeling of entering a medieval dungeon. After our eyes become accustomed to the darkness we can discern the long rows of stone piers which divide the interior into a series of domed chambers. Here and there shafts of diffuse sunlight enter through chinks in the vaulted ceiling, revealing the brilliant colours of the rugs and animal skins which cover the stone floor. As one walks through the mosque one comes upon groups of peasant women huddled together in the shadows. Some of them sit on the floor with their backs resting against the piers and gossip in rough country voices, while others pray quietly, rocking back and forth on their haunches. These women direct one to the *türbe* of Abu Sofyan, which is approached through a long, vaulted corridor which passes through a side wall of the dungeon. The end of the corridor is closed by an ornate iron grille, through which one can look into the interior of the tomb. The catafalque which covers the grave of Abu Sofyan lies in the centre of a large domed chamber which is illuminated by a single beam of moted sunlight which enters through a tiny window high in the dome above. This beam glows upon the gold-embroidered green cloth covering the catafalque of the saint and is reflected on to the whitewashed walls of the tomb, bathing them in a pale green light. The peasant women who come to pray at Abu Sofyan's *türbe* are quite ignorant of history and know of him only as a sainted prince who was martyred in the days of the Prophet. The sight of these veiled women praying in the shadows around the entrance to the tomb can evoke Biblical images.

Another medieval Arab hero-saint, Baba Cafer, is buried just across the Golden Horn, in the district of the Prison Gate. Baba Cafer, who was killed in the year 806 while on an embassy from Haroun-ul-Raschid to the Emperor Nicephorus I, is buried in one of the few remaining towers of the Byzantine sea-walls along the Golden Horn. This tower, which was called the Bagno, served for centuries as a prison, both under the Byzantines and the Ottoman Turks. According to Evliya Efendi:

> Cafer Baba was buried in a place within the prison of the infidels, where to this day his name is insulted by all the unbelieving male-factors, debtors, murders, etc. imprisoned there. But when (God be praised!) Istanbul was taken, the prison having likewise been captured, the grave of Cafer Baba in the tower of the Bagno became a place of pilgrimage which is visited by those who have been released from prison and call down blessings in opposition to the curses of the unbelievers.

The keeper of the tomb quoted these words as he directed us to the grave of Cafer Baba, which is located on the top floor of the tower. He related to us the circumstances of Cafer Baba's death, of how he was received by the Emperor in his palace and then thrown into the Bagno and treacherously murdered there. At the end of his tale the keeper paused for a moment as if searching for an appropriate moral lesson. Then his face brightened into a smile and he said to us, 'And in those days eggs were not fifty *kuruş* apiece!' We could only agree.

One of the best-loved of all Stamboul saints is Sheikh Vefa, who is known as the friend of the poor. Although Sheikh Vefa was one of the most renowned scholars in the time of the Conqueror and was well-versed in all of the seventy sciences, he decided quite early in life that he would devote himself entirely to the welfare of the poor. He therefore used his fortune to establish a pious foundation, which included a small mosque, an alms house, a public bath, a primary school, a han for travellers, and other charitable facilities. Within Sheikh Vefa's *külliye* the poor were assured of food, comfort and shelter for as long as they were in need. During the last years of his life Sheikh Vefa's devotion to them grew so intense that he refused to look upon any but the face of the poor. For that reason he once refused an invitation to dine with the young Sultan Beyazıt II, who had heard of his good works and wished to see him. This refusal greatly aroused the Sultan's curiosity, and after the Sheikh's death he ordered his tomb to be opened so that he could look upon Vefa's saintly face. Sheikh Vefa was buried in the garden of his pious foundation and his *türbe* was cared for by the poor, who continued to benefit from his charity long after his death. His *türbe* was for centuries a very popular shrine among the poor, but it is badly neglected and is rapidly falling into ruins. In the past few years, however, the poor of Stamboul have once again come to benefit from the Sheikh's charity. They have moved into the graveyard which surrounds his *türbe* and constructed their ramshackle huts there, moving the tombstones into the *türbe* and piling them around Vefa's catafalque. In this modest way, then, Sheikh Vefa continues to serve the poor in death as he did in life.

Another famous mystic-saint of the sixteenth century has still a considerable following among the people of Istanbul. This is Yahya Efendi, whose *türbe* is located in Beşiktaş, on a tree-shaded hillside over-looking the Bosphorus. Some of the most awful-looking beggars in town congregate around the entrance to the *türbe*, hardly a good advertisement for the renowned healing powers of the saint. Yahya Efendi was born in Trebizon at the same time as Süleyman the Magnificent, whom his mother nursed as an infant. After Süleyman became Sultan, Yahya Efendi followed him to Istanbul and built for himself a house on the spot where his tomb is now located. He there spent the remainder of his life writing religious poetry and in caring for the sick and the poor. According to Evliya Efendi: 'Yahya Efendi is buried on the top of a hill overlooking the sea; the four walls of his *türbe* are covered with the inscriptions of a hundred thousand divine lovers breathing out their feelings in verse. Even now he converses every Friday night with Hızırilyas, taking from him lessons in mysticism.'

It is quite fitting that the most unique of all of Istanbul's saints usually have no shrine at all. They possessed nothing when they were alive and their shades would probably feel imprisoned in tombs. These are the harmless and amusing lunatics whom Evliya refers to as the 'saint-fools, idiots and ecstatic or inspired men'. One might also include the *aptal,* or holy idiots, of whom there are said to be only seventy in the world at any one time; although an informal census would seem to indicate that Stamboul is inhabited by far more than that modest number. These characters are, of course, to be found at all times and in all towns, but nowhere are they tolerated and protected and indulged in their lunacies as they are in Istanbul, which is undoubtedly why they reach sainthood here so frequently. Here is Evliya Efendi's description of a few of the saint-fools of his time:

Divani Dokhani Kuster Dede was much given to the use of snuff and young boys amused themselves by filling his hand with dust instead, so that many times he snuffed up more than a hundred *derhems* of dust a day . . . Bülbül Divanesi [the Lunatic with the Nightingale] used to walk around carrying a cage with a nightingale in it that sang even in winter . . . Dabbağ Divanesi used to walk naked through the town and lived in winter in the Archery Field, sweating even in the deepest snow . . . Kisudar Mehmet Efendi walked about barefooted and bareheaded in both winter and summer. He wore but a coarse white cloth and carried a hatchet in his hand . . . Sumulki Dede had his station in the Hippodrome; if he threw bones to a man passing that person was sure to win that day some advantage in the Divan, but if he spat on him it was the contrary . . . Sabah Sabah is the sultan of all saint-fools. He used to spit large quantities of phlegm in the faces of those he disliked. He accompanied all parties of pleasure on shore and sea and raved night and day through the streets of Constantinople . . . Papas Dinavi, the mad priest of Galata. He was a merry fool with whose manners the whole world was pleased.

The Kisudar Mehmet Efendi mentioned above was actually present at Evliya's birth and at that time gave his hatchet to the infant as a present. 'I'll make a present of this to the boy,' he said, 'and it shall accompany him to many victories. By virtue of it he shall never be afraid of anything; and in his youth he shall play smoothly in the sand without hurting his hand against a stone.' Evliya tells us that he carried this hatchet with him on his many military campaigns, all of which he survived without harm, just as the saint-fool had prophesied.

The greatest of saint-fools in Evliya's time was the one they called Boynuzlu Divanesi, the Lunatic with the Horns. Here is Evliya's description of this madman and his amusing antics:

In the long days he used to sit upon the bridge at Kasımpaşa and s ay to all who passed '*Sallah*' (instead of *İnşallah*, if God pleases) 'you'll go to the Kaaba.' The wonder was that he knew men by their names, whom he had never seen before and saluted them as old acquaintances, and instantly remembered those whom he had not seen for twenty or thirty years, as well as the names of all their relations. His bosom was filled with horns of goats, gazelles and sheep. Merry fellows frequently went to try him, by saying, 'Ahmet, show me my horn!' If they happened to be married he would answer with some anecdote concerning their wives, and would give to some a small, to others a great horn from his collection. If the man who asked was not married he used to answer, 'Thy horn is not yet grown.' If someone said, 'Ahmet Dede, I'll give thee a horn, dance a little,' he would get up instantly, knock with the fingers of his right hand like a stork, and begin to dance like Venus in the sky, during which dance people brought him all kinds of horns. If you went to him a month afterwards and asked him where your horn was, he would put his hand into his bosom and show you the very same which you had given him. In brief, he was a light-hearted fool. Since he undertook the journey into Abyssinia and the country of the negroes, we have not heard of him.

Although three centuries have passed since Evliya's time the saint-fools are still to be seen on the streets of Istanbul. Two very well-known saint-fools work as *hamals*, carrying crates of produce from the markets along the Golden Horn. Each vies with the other in trying to achieve the most rapid delivery of his crates, and towards this purpose they have in their own mad ways tried to enlist the aid of modern technology. Solomon, known as the Chauffeur *Hamal*, has strapped to his chest a steering-wheel, gear-shift and hand-brake which he operates most efficiently as he speeds barefoot through the narrow streets of Galata. Yakob, the Flying *Hamal*, has tried to outdo Solomon by attaching a large aeroplane-propeller to the top of his load. Both Solomon and Yakob supplement these mechanical devices by making loud motor-noises with their mouths. Occasionally, the two of them come running together down the Street of Steps from Pera to Galata and we all back into doorways to avoid being trampled by these two barefooted madmen as they race one another to the Galata Bridge.

The most famous of present-day saint-fools is Şevki, the Lunatic Taxi-Driver. Şevki, who is also known as *Karincaezmez*, or the Man Who Will Not Kill Ants, is a devoted supporter of the Galatasaray football club. He dresses from head to foot in their orange and yellow colours and has painted his ancient taxi in the same hues, decorating it with signs and banners glorifying Galatasaray. His children are all named after members of the team and he dresses them and his poor wife in orange and yellow too. All patrons of his taxi must swear their allegiance to Galatasaray before they are allowed to get in. On the night before each game Şevki appears in Galatasaray Square holding his arms aloft in silent prayer for his team, fingering a string of huge orange and yellow prayer beads. Şevki's reputation as a saint is based partly on his concern for the safety of ants, but is mostly due to the gratitude of the many supporters of Galatasaray, the most popular and successful football team in town.

Two of the maddest of the holy idiots of our acquaintance would never have achieved sainthood anywhere but in Stamboul. They always make their first appearance at the beginning of spring, and when we see them we know that good times and good weather are ahead. They invariably appear together along the shores of the Bosphorus, but somehow they remain sublimely unaware of one another's existence. A bus has just stopped at the corner in Bebek, and who is that strange character getting out? Why it's the Bird of Night and he is swooping towards the Bosphorus in his black cape, ready to begin his daily flights along the shore between Bebek and Rumeli Hisar! And there, who is that hiding behind the *çınar* in Nazmi's café? It's the Colonel's Son, eyes glinting, laughing crazily, little wooden sword ready to duel stately and large-breasted lady strollers and later some mad directing of traffic in the square . . .

As Evliya wrote about the saints of his time: 'Some are nobles, some imbeciles, some distracted men, some holy men, some wise, some poor, some walk under the dress of the common people, some as sheikhs, and some as drunkards; for the tradition says: My saints are all under the vaults of heaven, nobody knows them but I.' Such are the saints of Stamboul, those of Evliya's time and of our own. They all await canonisation.

Carved wooden shutters

22

In the Days of the Dervishes

Throughout the *Seyahatname* Evliya Efendi lists the poets, mystics and divines of the various dervish orders which flourished in his time and before. In his descriptions of these saintly dervishes, Evliya reveals yet another aspect of the life of old Stamboul, this one, like so many others, now all but gone from the modern town. But, once again, Evliya evokes the vanished past and gives us a glimpse of what life was like here in the days of the dervishes.

The dervish movement was a reaction against the spiritual austerity of Islam and represented a desire for a more tangible religious experience. Each of the different dervish orders sought to attain communion with the divine in one way or another; some through contemplation and mysticism, others through the renunciation of worldly goods and the mortification of the flesh, and a few, like the Mevlevi and the Bektaşi, through the divine harmonies of music and dance. Whoever has heard the ethereal and haunting melodies of the Mevlevi, the famous whirling dervishes, will not soon forget them. And whoever has met a Bektaşi learns something of how the brotherhood of men could have been bound together by universal love, but never was.

The dervish communities lived in monasteries, or *tekkes*, where they could practise their devotions without distraction from the outside world. The dervish orders were banned and dispersed during the early years of the Turkish Republic and their *tekkes* are now abandoned and falling into ruins. There are scores of these silent buildings scattered around Istanbul, their windows smashed, their roofs gone, their walls half-fallen and overgrown with vines, their graveyards filled with weeds and rubbish. In their ghostly silence they are a poignant reminder of how, in the days of the dervishes, the town must have fairly hummed to the sound of their music and poetry as they sang and danced and played their way to paradise.

Evliya Efendi, who was himself a dervish for a time, evokes memories of those harmonious times in his description of the Mevlevi *tekke* in Beşiktaş:

> The Mevlevi *tekke* in Beşiktaş is only one storey high. The room for the dancing and singing of the dervishes looks out towards the sea. It is covered with a curious wooden roof, which our present architects would be unable to execute. The cells of the *fakirs* on the west side of the dancing-floor are of nut-tree wood and three sides are enclosed with windows. Their Sheikh, Hasan Dede, who was more than a hundred and ten years old at the time of his death, used to mount the chair on assembly days and, falling into ecstasy, would many times interpret the verses of the Mesnevi according to the author's original meaning. His successor, Nizen Dervish Yusuf Çelebi, would at times hurl himself down from his chair among the performing *fakirs*. When he sang, his voice was so inspired that his audience would remain spellbound. All the lovers of the deity would gather round him and listen to the divine chanting until they were completely out of their wits. He was a very prince of the speculative way of contemplation.

Our own village of Rumeli Hisar is most richly blessed with the tombs and graves of holy dervishes, although their *tekkes* have long since vanished. One of the most venerated of these saints is Durmuş Dede, whose tombstone stands in a forlorn little graveyard beside the Bosphorus, in a once lovely garden now overshadowed by high-rise apartments. Durmuş Dede was a dervish-seer who lived in a *tekke* on this spot early in the seventeenth century. He was of great assistance to mariners, for he would advise the captains of passing boats as to whether or not the omens were favourable for their voyage. The sailors repaid his good advice by leaving him an *okka* of meat whenever they sailed by his house. An old boatman in the village informed me that this custom continued up until the early years of the present century, with the divinatory service perpetuated by Bektaşi dervishes who lived in a little *tekke* near Durmuş Dede's grave. This holy garden also contains the graves of Sheikh İsmail Çelebi and his disciples, of whom Evliya Efendi has this marvellous tale to tell: 'The Emperor was at Kandilli, when the bodies of the Sheikh and his disciples were thrown into the sea at Constantinople by the Stable Gate. He and his ten followers came floating down the Bosphorus to Kandilli, dancing on the waves with their heads in their hands. The Emperor's suite seeing this miracle represented to him that they must have been unjustly executed. The Emperor then began to weep as he watched them floating against the current to the opposite shore at Rumeli Hisar, where they were buried at the foot of Durmuş Dede, and for the ten days following light was seen pouring down on their graves.'

Many of our village saints are buried in a picturesque graveyard high above Rumeli Hisar, on top of that grassy knoll called Evliyalar Tepesi, the Hill of the Saints. This was the site of the oldest of all the dervish *tekkes* in Istanbul, founded in 1452 by Bedrettin Baba, a Bektaşi dervish in the army of Mehmet the Conqueror. Bedrettin Baba's tombstone can still be seen there, along with those of the long line of sainted *şeyh* who directed the *tekke* until it was finally closed in the year 1925. One of the best-loved of these *şeyh* was Nafi Baba, who died during the First World War and was buried behind the *tekke* by a squad of German soldiers who staffed an artillery post there. Although Nafi Baba has been dead now for more than half a century, there are still many fond memories of him in the village of Rumeli Hisar. An old Armenian lady told me that when she was a small girl she often saw Nafi Baba riding on his white mule up the cobbled lanes of the village to his *tekke* on the hill. She remembers that he had a long white beard and was dressed in a white robe and wore an enormous white turban on his head. His progress through the village was always slow and joyous, for Nafi Baba stopped to bless each doorway that he passed and distributed sweets to all the children who came flocking around him. His memory is still honoured, for each year Nafi Baba's descendants gather together for a picnic on the Hill of the Saints on the anniversary of his death. I was once

privileged to attend one of these dervish family-reunions, having been
invited there by my good friend, Ali Artemel, Nafi Baba's grandnephew.
That day I had the honour of meeting Nusset Baba, the last *şeyh* of the
tekke before its closure, and was also introduced to Güllü Hanım, one of
the last surviving women dervishes. Güllü Hanım, who although now in
her eighties still shows evidence of her youthful beauty, was captured in
a slave-raid in the Caucasus when she was a young girl and was sold to a
pasha in Stamboul. She loathed the pasha and the life she was forced to
live with him and soon managed to escape from his harem, finding
refuge in the Bektaşi *tekke* on the Hill of the Saints. Güllü Hanım lived
there happily until the *tekke* was closed and then she moved with some
of her friends and relatives to a house in Rumeli Hisar, where she still
lives today. When the picnic ended, Ali and I, together with Nusset
Baba, Güllü Hanım and all of the others at the picnic, drank a toast in
red wine to the blessed memory of all the departed dervishes on the Hill
of the Saints.

And afterwards we walked down to Nazmi's café on the seaside, as we
so often do late on a spring afternoon. We were sitting there, sipping our
rakı and watching the last golden reflections of sunset in the windows
across the Bosphorus, when a merry old character walked across the
road and sat on the wall beside our table. He had a snow-white beard and
bright blue eyes, wore a ragged turban and a shepherd's cloak, and was
shod in sandals fashioned from slices of automobile tyres. 'Good day,
my friends,' he said to us, 'I wish you good appetite.' 'Would you join us
in our meal, Baba?' said Ali to the old man. 'Thank you, my son,' said he,
'I would appreciate a little bread and cheese, for I have walked a long way
today and have not eaten since morning.' 'How far have you come, Baba?'
asked Ali. 'I have walked all the way from Gumuşhane' (a town far in the
east of Turkey), he said, 'and I have come to say my prayers at the *türbe* of
my old *şeyh*, Nuri Baba, who is buried beside our *tekke* in Kasımpaşa. I
have not been to Stamboul for many, many years, and now I have come
to pay one last visit before I die.' Then, after having eaten, he laughed
heartily and told us that we were a fine group of gentlemen who were
enjoying life in the manner of dervishes. 'Would you join us in a bottle

of wine, Baba?' said Ali, well aware of the fabled habit of the Bektaşi sect, of which our guest was surely a member. The old dervish smacked his lips and laughed. 'That is very kind of you, my son, but it is my custom to drink wine only with the best intentions, and since my intentions at the moment are not of the very highest I must decline, most reluctantly.' Then he got down from the café wall and bowed to us, thanking us for our kind hospitality to an old man, and bade us goodbye. 'When will we see you again, Baba?' called Ali after him. The old Bektaşi laughed and said, 'We will all see each other one day in paradise, *inşallah*!' and then waved back to us as he walked off down the twilit Bosphorus road.

The oldest of the dervish *tekkes* still standing in Istanbul is that of İskender Paşa, which was founded in old Pera in 1492. Having heard that the *tekke* had recently been restored and was now open to the public, I went there one day to inspect it. When I arrived I found that the rumour was only half-true, for although the *tekke* had been restored it was still closed, and a sign warned me that I should not enter. But Stamboul signs are posted mostly to be ignored, and so I decided to enter anyway. And by this fortunate decision I was transported for a few brief moments to the Stamboul of Evliya's time.

When I entered the *tekke* I was pleased to see how splendidly it had been restored; for there was the polished nut-wood floor where the whirling dervishes danced their spinning way to ecstasy, the stage where once sat the company of dervish musicians playing haunting melodies on the *ney*, or Turkish flute, the screened gallery from whence the Sultan and his court observed the dancers.

When I had finished my tour an old gentleman came over and asked me if I would care to come outside in the garden and have a glass of tea with him and his friends. I thanked him and said yes, and he led me to a grape-arbor beside the *tekke*. There were three other ancients sitting there and they greeted me with almost ceremonious courtesy. I could sense immediately that there was something quite out of the ordinary about these old men; their manners were so gentle and their faces so serene; their speech an older and more archaic Turkish. And then one of them produced a *ney* and began to play, while another sang a most lovely song which I soon recognised to be a *mesnevi*, one of the mystical verses of the Mevlana. From this I recognised that my companions were Mevlevi dervishes, singing and playing once again in the garden of their old *tekke*. I later learned that they were presently residing in Konya, where once a year they were permitted to perform their ancient rites on the feast day of their founder, Mevlana Jelal-ud-din Rumi. When the dervishes finished their song I complimented them and then I quoted these lines from Evliya's *Seyahatname* concerning the playing of the *ney*: 'The divines of Rum hold the playing of this instrument not to be forbidden by the law, because it was played before the great mystic Mevlana Jelal-ud-din, and it is even now played in all the *tekkes* of the Mevlevi. On the night of the Prophet's nuptials the half-drum, the *ney* and the violin were played, and therefore these instruments continue to be played in the *tekke* of the dervishes.'

The old dervishes were very taken by this and were at the same time curious that a foreigner should have read Evliya Efendi's *Seyahatname*. Then the *ney*-player asked me if I knew that Evliya Efendi was buried nearby. I was very surprised at this, for I had always thought that Evliya had died and been buried in Edirne, and so I told the old dervish of my doubts. He replied, 'It is true that Evliya Efendi spent most of his later years in Edirne, my son, but he left there in about his seventieth year to undertake a voyage to Egypt and the Holy Land. On his return from that journey he settled once again in Stamboul and soon afterwards died and was buried alongside his ancestors, or so I have been told.' I asked him if he knew just where Evliya might be buried. He answered, 'According to tradition, Evliya Efendi is interred in the old burial-ground of Meyyitzade in the district of Kasımpaşa, only a short distance from our *tekke*.' I told him that I was very anxious to find Evliya's grave, for he and his *Seyahatname* had for many years been my guide to Stamboul, and I would now like to pay my respects to his memory in the place where he had been laid to rest. The old dervishes appreciated this sentiment and wished me God's blessing as I stood up to leave, inviting me to come again and join them whenever I was passing by. I replied

A child in Sulukule, the gypsy neighbourhood

that I would surely do so, and then bade them farewell for a time, thanking them for their kindness and hospitality.

As I walked towards Kasımpaşa, I wondered if Evliya was really buried at Meyyitzade as the old dervish said. And I was also puzzled by the very name of Meyyitzade, the Son of the Dead, for it seemed to make no sense. But then I recalled the fantastic tale which Evliya told of Meyyitzade and of how he acquired this strange name:

Meyyitzade's tomb: Before going to the siege of Erla his father recommended the child, then in his mother's womb, to the care of God Almighty. Soon after his departure the woman died and was buried; she then gave birth in the tomb and nourished her child by a miracle. The father on his return, having heard of his wife's death, desired to be shown the grave, where he found the child still living and suckled by his mother's breast. He praised God and took the child home, who became a great and learned man; he died in the time of Ahmet I and was again buried close to his mother. A cupola was erected over the grave, which is a place of general pilgrimage. Near it are buried my father Dervish Mehmet Zilli, and his mother, as well as my grandfather Timurci Kara Ahmet, and my grandfather Yavuz Ali Uzbeg and innumerable relations of mine, poor Evliya. I offer a prayer for them!

When I arrived in Kasımpaşa I made enquiries about the Meyyitzade burial-ground, but no one seemed to know of its whereabouts. An old Jewish gentleman told me that this whole area had once been a cemetery, the Petit Champs des Morts, but that it had all been built over many years ago. The only tomb I could see was an ancient, half-ruined *türbe*, which stood beside the road running down to the Golden Horn. I began walking towards the *türbe* and then, to my astonishment, I saw on a street-sign that the name of the road was – the Avenue of Evliya Çelebi! I found the door to the *türbe* open and walked inside, feeling that I had finally reached the end of my search. But the only tombstones I could find within the *türbe* were marked with the names of Katip Mehmet Çelebi and Saliha Hatun, and the dates of their deaths, 1542 and 1685.

An old inscription on the outside of the *türbe* stated that this was the tomb of Lagusa Kadin, that is, the Lady Who Has Given Birth, indicating that this was undoubtedly the tomb which Evliya described, where took place the fabulous birth of Meyyitzade, the Son of the Dead.

But of Evliya Efendi's grave I could find no trace, and so my quest finally ended in disappointment. And thus Evliya's only monument in Istanbul is a street-sign which bears his name, on an avenue which perhaps passes over his unmarked grave. But as I walked back towards Pera along the Avenue of Evliya Çelebi, I realised that there could be no more fitting monument to him, who spent his life strolling along the streets of Stamboul.

The Passage of Flower

23

The Passage of Flowers

It is said that on a certain day in June the crazy tilt of the buildings allows the sun briefly into this alley. Between solstices it gets its light second-hand; from slime-silvered cobbles and from shining marble table-tops awash with beer. Osman Efendi passed by here an age ago and his delight in what he saw was such that the alley has been named for him. The Street of Osman Efendi Passed By leads from the flower-market to the fish-bazaar by way of an arcade lined with *meyhanes*, or kerbside taverns, and is therefore a museum of Stamboul smells. It is more often called the Çiçek Pasaji, the Passage of Flowers.

The *meyhanes* of the Passage are the favourite haunts of the *Akşamcılar*, the Evening Drinkers, who can be seen there daily draining giant glasses of beer called Argentines. The Evening Drinkers, who on occasion have been known to drink in the afternoon and in the morning too, usually sit at long marble tables inside these *meyhanes*. In good weather they move out into the alley itself, taking their meals from the tops of beer barrels. Some prefer the Church, a spacious tavern hung with rococo chandeliers, but I prefer the Senate because the talk is best there. The Senate is in session throughout the day, but more important affairs are discussed in the evening, after the sun has set and steel shutters come crashing down in the shops around town. This nocturnal congress is illuminated by coloured lights, protected by pendant talismans, and presided over by a bored and omniscient cashier.

The *meyhane* kitchens perch on the upper floors of the taverns. Swarthy, unshaven cooks lean out from smoke-spewing windows and gossip with their friends across the alley, commenting on the deformities of the strollers, whistling at passing girls, now and then disappearing into their cave-like kitchens when waiters rush out into the Passage shouting up orders from the taverns below. I sometimes amuse myself by walking quickly through the Passage, calling out the names of all my favourite dishes, and then sitting quietly at a beer barrel while waiters run about looking for the gentlemen who ordered the stuffed mussels, the grilled mullet, the shish-kebab, the fried brains. Once accusing fingers were pointed at me and I was forced to eat it all, and did so with pleasure.

The Turkish meal is a long and unhurried ceremony; a procession of delicacies carried by platoons of staggering waiters; irrigated with rakı, that soul-satisfying, intellect-deadening, national anise drink; and, above all, accompanied by talk. The talk is continuous, loud and passionate; emphasised and punctuated by ritual hand-gestures; illustrated by dramatic facial expressions; all pronouncements requiring exclamations of agreement, disagreement, astonishment or disbelief; all tipsy speeches applauded with roars of laughter and an exchange of rough embraces and bristly kisses; followed by a glass-clinking toast and a bellowed order for more food and drink. Exhausted waiters in unlaced shoes shuffle to the table with yet another tray of 'Belly-Split-Open', a sweet plate of 'The Lady's Navel', a savoury dish of 'The Imam Fainted', a girth-expanding mound of *zerde pilavı*, that favourite dish of eunuchs and Janissaries, and one more round of rakı. And when they have had their fill of food, these stout men sing to one another soft and quavering Turkish love songs. Late at night, as they sway together at their long tables, the *Akşamcılar* resemble apostles at a drunken sacrament.

Istanbul is best seen from a seat by a tavern window in the Passage of Flowers, froth-crowned Argentine in hand. The city is at heart nothing more than the sum of its citizens, and most of these will eventually stroll by your window or sit next to you, drinking an Argentine themselves. You will get to know the Stamboullus in this way, and later you can visit them in the monuments they inhabit. This is the Levantine approach to sightseeing, a distinct improvement on the *Guide Bleu*.

The Stamboullus pass by with their hands clasped behind their backs, fingering worry-beads. Their faces are seamed, furrowed, wrinkled, weathered and warted; their hooded eyes rheumy, bloodshot and jaundiced; their hooked and hairy-nostrilled noses dripping beads of snot; their hat brims turned down and their collars up; their long, black, shroud-like overcoats skimming the muddy pavement; walking with the lurching, stumbling gait produced by a lifetime on cobblestones. They stroll through the Passage slowly, staring into the taverns without apparent interest, turning their massive bodies rather than their immobile heads, occasionally crashing into one another and rebounding impassively, then continuing on their aimless way. The hours pass as I review this drab parade, and grey afternoon changes imperceptibly into grey-blue evening. For there are no clocks in town and the light in the Passage is too diffuse to give the hour. The weather is known from the shine on the cobbles and the season from the dress of the strollers.

But I know that twilight has ended when I see the night people of Stamboul beginning to make their appearance in the Passage. There are itinerant pedlars: sellers of hepatitic shellfish, uncrackable nuts, timeless wristwatches, second-hand shoes with the backs folded down for easy removal in mosques, worn overcoats still warm from their last owners, horoscopes for the unlucky and zodiacal lapel-pins for the star-crossed and superstitious. There are wandering mendicants: beggars deaf, dumb, blind, legless, armless, or with thickets of twisted limbs; along with widows, orphans, veterans and abandoned patriarchs. There are Gypsies: leading bears, playing fiddles, beating tambourines, pounding drums, dancing, singing, begging, pimping and pilfering, their dark eyes always alert for the possibilities of plunder. A drunken painter sells landscapes of an arcadia which can be reached only after a long trip on cheap wine. A hairy peasant sells chances on gaunt chickens which are always won by another hairy peasant who is undoubtedly his brother. A purple-eyed prostitute offers to measure our blood-pressure, which does not rise at the sight of her elephantine charms. A prick-eared dwarf limps by using a tree-branch for a cane, striking out at the tormenting Gypsy boys who pluck at his rags. A hunchbacked crone stops for a thimbleful of beer and hands a passionate love note to Ali, the handsome young barman . . . One evening, while we were drinking by candlelight during a power failure, a swift ancient came running through the Passage and sold a whole carton of cigarette-lighters; he assured us that they had been just recently stolen by him. At the sound of police whistles from the fish-bazaar we put out our candles to assist the old thief in his escape. Then, upon the arrival of the blundering police, we flicked our lighters on and off to illuminate the comic chase as in a silent movie, while the Passage echoed with cheers and derisive laughter.

When the evening is at its height our joy is momentarily withered by the appearance of a cigarette-seller with unfocused and uncoordinated eyes, one orb apparently fixed on hell and the other on paradise. We quickly buy his cigarettes so that he will leave, after which we touch our amulets to ward off the evil-eye before resuming our conversations.

And although he has been standing in the doorway for hours, we do not notice until late in the evening the bankrupt belt-seller, Mad Ahmet. Swathed to the eyes in a black muffler, he peers through his matted tangles of hair and beard and stands dreaming in a hashish cloud while his belts are stolen by Gypsies. He buys the belts back later at a loss, but being demented he is not aware of the unfair exchange and so is not disturbed. The more cynical of the *Akşamcılar* say that he is a police spy.

Each evening new and eccentric characters appear upon the scene. An acrobat stands on his head in the centre of the Passage. He walks upon his hands along the tops of beer barrels to my window. His earrings dangle beside his swarthy, upside-down face and I notice that he has a purple star tattooed on his forehead. I attempt to engage him in conversation but he silently takes my coin and leaves, walking along the Passage on his hands, hardly noticed by the strollers. A young man seated across the table lifts his Argentine to me and smiles. He has a darkly handsome face and the chest and shoulders of a young Apollo. He finishes his beer and bids me good evening, after which he climbs down from his stool and disappears. A moment afterwards I see him in the alley as he turns and waves back to me, a bisected demigod striding on his stumps over the cobbles of the Passage.

As the evenings go by, I watch for the unpredictable transits of Arnaut Mehmet, the Albanian flower-pedlar. At times he is not seen for many months and I am told in the taverns that he is dead. Others who know him better say that he is wandering in the lower depths of Istanbul and that we will see him again when he has run his course. For this bum has the unerring sense of season of a migratory bird, and resurrects each spring along with the flowers he sells, like a drunken phoenix. We know that he is back when we hear his familiar shout – 'Rose! Rose!' – as he staggers into the Passage from the fish-market, swinging his bouquets about him to clear a path through the throng. Totally and unredeemably drunk, his forehead deeply creased from an axe-blow, bloodshot eyes burning in his grimy face, nose busted, teeth shattered and lips swollen from his violent encounters in the underworld, grey-haired chest showing through the torn shirt and tattered suit which have been stained by every foul alley in Istanbul, ragged trousers held up by a piece of frayed rope and the seat ripped out as if by a mad dog, pant legs ripped and flapping in the breeze, black toes protruding from the shards of shoes which he must have fought for with an alley-cat, his body caked with dirt and stinking like a leprous rat, he has, nonetheless, a certain dignity about him. Standing now before my window, the Albanian offers me a rose from his bouquet and bows from the waist when I present him a double rakı in return. He downs the rakı in one gulp, smacks his lips appreciatively, and then smashes the empty glass on his head before continuing along the Passage. He now feels fit to resume his flower-peddling and approaches lady shoppers with a charming but incoherent speech and what he believes to be his most patrician manner. But when they see and smell this drunken, reeking apparition the ladies invariably flee, while the Albanian stumbles through the crowd in angry pursuit, hurling his roses after them, bellowing in what I imagine must be Montenegrin. When the ladies make good their escape to the safety of the main street, the Albanian, now rose-less, shrugs his shoulders and staggers sadly back through the Passage. Stopping once again before my window, he bows to me and his ruined face brightens in an angelic smile. I buy him another double rakı, which he quaffs with the same ceremonial shattering as before. Then he bows again, twirls his cap around on his scarred head, and staggers off down the Passage shouting – 'Rose! Rose!' – that unconquerable spirit. The Albanian is always followed in his wanderings by two furtive and stumbling figures, even more ruinous than he, who steal his roses from him, picking them up after he has thrown them all over the Passage in his wild career. And there are others, I am sure, who depend on these two in turn, living off them in some dark corner of this fantastic town.

After the Albanian has gone, a wandering minstrel enters the Passage through the fish-market gate. He strums a few chords on his saz and is then called to play for a group of old friends sitting together at a beer barrel. The minstrel sits with them and plays while the old men sing plaintive Anatolian ballads centuries old. When the old men have finished their songs and toasted one another with one last rakı, the minstrel bids them good-night and sings a traditional parting-song. Then he leaves too, and I hear the echo of his voice as he wanders off to play in the *meyhanes* of the fish-bazaar, still singing of unrequited love.

And as I sit alone by the tavern window I recall the words which Evliya Efendi wrote so long ago, speaking of the wandering minstrels of his time: 'These players are possessed of the particular skill to evoke by their tones the remembrance of absent friends and distant countries, so that their hearers grow melancholy.' And Evliya's words evoke for me the memory of the dear friends who once sat with me in the Passage, most of them now far away and some of them gone for ever, and so I grow melancholy too. Then I think of Evliya himself, who for so long has been my unseen companion in my strolls through Stamboul, and I wonder what he would say if he could see his beloved town today, so changed but so much the same, and then I lift a last glass in his memory.

Thus the evenings pass and the years go by in the Passage of Flowers, a little alleyway in Stamboul.

Afterword

It began, my father tells me, with the book his grandmother used to teach him how to read. It was called *A Pictorial Journey Around the World,* and in between its illustrations of the American West and a voyage up the Limpopo, there was an engraving of Constantinople.

How that book came to be in the small seaside village in the West of Ireland where my father spent his early childhood was another story. And that story began in Constantinople. In 1855, after he was

The author in the 1960s

wounded in the Siege of Sevastopol, my great-great-grandfather Thomas Ashe was sent to Florence Nightingale's hospital in Scutari on the city's Asian shore. He bought this book before boarding the ship that took him home. He didn't know how to read, but he put this right by marrying the postmistress, who did. *A Pictorial Journey Around the World* went on to become the family primer.

My father had already crossed the Atlantic Ocean once by the time he learned how to read. He would cross it three more times before he was seven. During his time in the US Navy in World War II, he made nine more crossings. On his nineteenth birthday, he was in a gun nest in the South Pacific, shooting up at Japanese planes. From there he sailed across the Indian Ocean to Calcutta, and through Burma on the top of

a train, arriving in China just as the World War ended and the Chinese
civil war began. The vessel he took home was the first warship to go
through the just-reopened Suez Canal. But it was, he tells me, that
pictorial journey that planted in his mind the idea of a life spent travelling,
and the engraving of Constantinople that promised something more.

It was a navy chaplain (to whom he had gone for books, he assures
me, and not religion) who gave my father the catalogue for the St John's
College Great Books Program. The list began with the *Odyssey* and the
Iliad and carried on through the centuries, and it took him the rest of the
war to get through it. He was restlessly at home again, in Brooklyn, New
York, pondering the last great book, Joyce's *Ulysses*, when he met my
mother. He tells me that he knew he was getting somewhere with her
when he went to the public library a few days later to find her taking out
some of the classics he had recommended. Neither came from the sort
of family that sent its children to university. It was thanks to the GI Bill
that my father was able to continue his education. My mother wasn't so
lucky, but by the time my father was awarded a doctorate in physics, she
had gone through the Great Books of St John several times over.

By now there were five of us. My brother was a year old when we
moved from Princeton, New Jersey to Istanbul in 1960. My sister was
five, and I was eight. And though my father had been reading us
adventure stories at bedtime for as long as I could remember, and at the
end of each chapter spinning the globe to see how many countries we
could identify by name and shape, nothing could have prepared me for
the dusty and cacophonous splendour that awaited us.

The Bosphorus campus that was to be our home was hushed and
green, offering us some respite, but we had not been at Robert College
for more than a week before we began our Saturday strolls through the
Old City. We would take the 8 o'clock ferry from Bebek and travel
down the Bosphorus, darting back and forth between the wooded hills
of Europe and Asia, until the skyline turned thick with minarets and
towers, domes and car exhaust, and horses, and donkeys and men in
dirty brown suits carrying furniture twice their size. Arriving at the edge
of the Galata Bridge, we would join the hordes to push and shove our

way across rotting, wobbling planks onto land that never felt quite as firm as I longed for it to be.

Eminönü in those days was a large open space without road markings or traffic lights. Pedestrians would walk in front of cars expecting them to stop, and if they could see you, they usually did. They could not help but notice my father, with my brother on his shoulders, and my mother at his side. But the only time they could see my sister and me was when we raced after our fast-disappearing parents, waving our arms wildly, and crying 'Slow down! Slow down!'

On our first walk, my father decided we should do the full circuit of the ancient city walls. I do not remember the bedraggled shores of the Golden Horn except that we went on and on, down cobblestone streets speckled with piles of manure that were sometimes dry and dusty, and sometimes still steaming. Almost all the houses were wooden, and unpainted, and disintegrating. The dogs lurking in packs outside them were not always friendly. There was hardly a window that did not frame an old lady, smiling and fingering her headscarf as she watched us pass. On every step and doorway there sat a mangy cat. The coffee-houses were packed with men rolling dice and snapping down their back-gammon pieces, while outside small boys played noisy, dusty games amongst the dogs and donkeys and horse carts, and small girls shouted down at them through lines of laundry. We passed a mosque with a courtyard where men were lining up to wash their feet and hands in a marble fountain. Around the corner was a larger fountain of gnarled and darkened marble that looked like a house. Towering above us was an aqueduct, and then a ruin that turned out to be a very hot church, and sometimes we could see the crumbling walls we were tying to follow, and sometimes we couldn't. Then suddenly there before us were the sea walls, strung with laundry and crawling with children. But we were not, warned my father, to be fooled by the trees growing out of some of its holes, and the stovepipes growing out of others. These walls had seen the rise and fall of two great empires, and assaults from the peoples of Europe and Asia.

As we dragged our tired, swollen feet along the Sea of Marmara, he told us their names. There were the Byzantines and the Greeks, the Ottomans and the Arabs and the Slavs and the Latin Empire, the Venetians and the Fourth Crusade. There was only a mile or two to go now before we rounded the last point to the ferry that would take us home. But just down the hill from the Blue Mosque, my sister walked into a lamppost. So instead of completing the circle, we went into an old fisherman's restaurant called *Kar ma Sen*, which means None of Your Business.

I did not know then that we had an invisible companion ushering us to the table. It was not until much later that my father told me that the first book he took out of our college library during his first week on campus was the 1834 translation by Joseph van Hammer of Evliya Çelebi's *Seyahatname*. One of Evliya's finest boasts was that he was the first and only man to have walked the full length of the city walls. He had done so, he claimed, in 1636, just after Murat IV opened a road along the sea walls. Within three months, the sea had washed the road away. But oh, the marvels Evliya had witnessed, only days before it was too late!

On every street of the city, my father tells me – and inside every monument, courtyard and museum, every church and mosque, every coffee-house and tavern and hole-in-the-wall shop – he has witnessed sights and scenes that Evliya described four centuries ago. His ghost, he says, is still at his side. It was Evliya who taught him how to see the city.

Or rather, it was Evliya who taught him to see what was no longer there. After two thousand years as a great world capital, Byzantium-Constantinople-Istanbul had become the second city in a struggling new republic that most of the world had trouble locating on a map. There was next to no tourism. The most recent guidebook on our shelves at home was published the year my father was born. That, I think, is why he first began to set down accounts of the walks he and my mother took first with us, and then with a growing circle of friends, colleagues and students, amongst them Sedat Pakay who was still in his teens back then. After taking many thousands of photographs during his walks with my father, he went on to study with Walker Evans at the Yale

University School of Fine Arts, and his work now hangs in museums all over the world. In the photographs he has so kindly granted permission to include here, you can see Evliya in every shadow.

By the late 1960s, my father's account of his travels with Evliya had turned into a thousand-page manuscript entitled *The Broken-Down Paradise*. It still sits in his study in three ring binders. Though it has never been published, it formed the basis of much of what you have read here. It was also one of two books that went on to form the basis of *Strolling through Istanbul*, first published by Redhouse Press in Istanbul in 1972 and now widely regarded as a classic.

His co-author – my Latin teacher – was Hilary Sumner-Boyd, who had in his youth been the secretary (and according to A. J. Ayer, perhaps the only member) of the Oxford Trotskyist Society, later serving as the business manager of Trotskyist journal *The Red Flag*, which he ran out of his flat in the Edgware Road. After saying goodbye to all that and defecting to Istanbul and Robert College in 1943, Hilary made the acquaintance of one Sven Larsen, professor of history of at the college. During his earlier years at the college, Larsen had worked with Alexander van Millingen, who had, along with the college librarian, Caspar Tügil, helped to build what was then considered one of the finest Near East collections in the world. It was to set down what van Millingen had taught Larsen, and what Larsen had taught him, that Hilary Sumner-Boyd had produced his own thousand-page book, a scholarly account of the city's long-neglected monuments. This, too, remains unpublished, though its pages went on to inspire many others, most notably Godfrey Goodwin's *A History of Ottoman Architecture*.

Together these friends walked miles and miles each Saturday. But it was never just the monuments, my father wishes to remind me. Every city walk included detours to Greek taverns and seaside cafés and Pera beer halls and restaurants run by retired Russian ballerinas. On the many occasions I tagged or was dragged along, I would be drinking *gazoz* or *Kola Koka* (and not *rakı* or beer or lemon vodka or the 2-lira Turkish champagne my parents and their friends took up to the dome of Aghia Irini Church for one of their more daring illicit picnics) and that may be why I remember many of the characters described in these pages better than anyone except, perhaps, my father.

By the time *Stamboul Sketches* was published in 1974, many of these characters had already vanished from the streets, and so, too, had many of the beer halls and taverns they'd once haunted. And by then, I had moved on, too. It was too heart-breaking, to stand by and watch all those beautiful wooden houses fall into themselves or burn to the ground, because their owners wanted to build themselves uglier and more profitable apartment blocks; to see the old caiques pulled out of the sea and the ferries thinning out, so that fuming minibuses could poison the air and clog up all the city streets; to look over at Asia from the European shores of the Bosphorus and see one great expanse of concrete, where there had once been wooded hills. For many years, I couldn't bear to go back.

When, in the early 1990s, I finally found the courage, my father took me back to the old city, to retrace some of our old steps. The wooden houses were almost all gone by then, as were the children of the sea walls, and the donkeys and horse carts and most of the cobblestones. In their place were cars and more cars, concrete and more concrete. And tourist shops, tourist hotels, tourist restaurants and tourist signs, amid the churches, mosques and monuments that had been cleaned and shined for them. But as we darted in and out of the old city walls, Evliya's ghost stayed with us, every step of the way. For here was the mosque to which he'd travelled by rowboat across the Golden Horn, after his vision of the Prophet in 1631. Over there was street named after him. And there, just up there, right across from the Sublime Porte, was the room in the Alay Köskü, where Evliya had almost certainly stood in 1638 to watch the last great procession of the Guilds. And as my father conjured it up for me, guild by guild, I at last understood what he had learned from our constant companion: the past is always with us, but not in what we see. It's in the story, and the beautiful voice telling it.

Maureen Freely
2014